To Minerv
      from Oie + family
   Christmas 1987

I know you don't need it
but thought it might be
fun to have. (If you have
it already give it back
and I'll find you some-
thing else!).

CAKE MAKING
& DECORATING

CAKE MAKING & DECORATING

BARBARA MAHER

Exeter Books

NEW YORK

ACKNOWLEDGEMENTS FROM THE AUTHOR

With thanks to Uta Schumacher-Voelker for her inspiration and the loan of innumerable books as reference; to Georgina Milne for typing a barely legible manuscript; to Valerie Cheney for her valuable assistance in the kitchen; to Maria Wosiek for coping with my household; to James Stewart who took the photographs for the book; and finally, to Barker Ellis Silver company for the loan of their silverware for photographic use.

A QUARTO BOOK

Copyright © 1984 Quarto Publishing
Limited
This edition first published in USA 1984
by Exeter Books
Distributed by Bookthrift
Exeter is a registered trademark of Simon
& Schuster
Bookthrift is a registered trademark of
Simon & Schuster, New York, New York
ISBN 0-671-06929-2

This book was designed and produced by
Quarto Publishing
32 Kingly Court
London W1

Art Director Jane Willis
Editorial Director Christopher Fagg
Designer Dave Allen
Editor Lydia Derbyshire
Photographer James Stewart

Typeset by Leaper & Gard Ltd, Bristol
Color origination by Universal Color Scanning Ltd, Hong Kong
Printed by Leefung Asco Printers Limited, Hong Kong

Contents

Introduction

The history of European cakes and baked sweetmeats begins in the Middle East. Early records show that the Ancient Egyptians baked over 40 kinds of spiced breads and pastries made from honey, milk and eggs, and prettily shaped in the form of birds, animals and obelisks.

The civilizations of the Middle East, and later of Greece and Rome, formed a great market for the spices and flavors brought by land and sea along the Spice Road from China, India and Ceylon. This trade came to be dominated by the Arabs and, with the spread of Islam, the Eastern Mediterranean developed a distinctive Arab style of spiced sweetmeats and delicacies.

For centuries after the fall of the Roman empire, northern Europe was cut off from the Mediterranean world. But, during the eleventh century, Crusaders from Europe rediscovered the delights of Middle Eastern cuisine, and took the recipes and ingredients back to their European homelands — beginning a tradition which continues to this day in the spiced cake and mince pies baked at Christmas time.

Monasteries played a major role too in the development of European baking. Despite the difficult, often violent, times of the Middle Ages, the monks continued to grow their own produce, cultivating herbs, vegetables and fruit trees; they also kept bees, sheep and other domestic animals. The monks also experimented with the new ingredients brought back by the crusaders, and their cooking and baking gained a fine reputation — their spiced honey cakes were particularly popular.

Meanwhile in Italy, Venice emerged as the major market for trade with the Orient. Italy became the channel for the exotic cooking techniques of the East. From the Arabs the Italians learned to make a wide range of sweets and desserts — ice creams, sorbets, and *dolci* based on honey, almond paste and cane sugar, or plain dough covered in syrup.

In 1553 Caterina de Medici journeyed from Florence to France for her marriage to the future King Henry II, bringing with her a team of expert cooks and pastry cooks. In this way the French were introduced to the new Italian style of cooking and baking, with its oriental inspiration. However, in the short term, the Italians remained firmly established as the leaders of European cookery, with an authoritative cookery book appearing in Italy little more than 30 years later. In this classic cookery book, the author Bartolomeo Scappi included nearly 1000 recipes, ranging from meat, poultry and fish to instructions on how to prepare pastry in the Arabic fashion. Numerous other pastries were also introduced — even the traditional 'pasta frollo' (short pastry) makes an early entrance here. In addition, Scappi illustrated, in meticulous detail, implements and kitchen utensils, many of which are still in use today. Yet within 50 years of this book, the initiative passed to the French chefs. Cooking and baking increased in importance and came to be considered as one of the civilized arts. Pastries, cakes, sweets, cream puffs, ices and cheesecakes now appeared at aristocratic European tables, and Paris and the royal court set the standard that all the major cities of Austria, Hungary, Germany, Switzerland, Spain and Britain tried to emulate.

At the same time, the foundation of a 'bourgeois' cuisine, with peasant overtones, was developing in less wealthy kitchens, using more basic and cheaper ingredients and fewer of the luxury items. Bread doughs enriched with honey or nuts and just a little spice; potato, mashed or dried and ground to replace the costly white flour —

any produce the land had to offer cheaply was of use. Spices and nuts were generally only used for festive and holy day bakery.

During the eighteenth century, coffee, tea and chocolate became the fashionable beverages of the upper classes. Baked confections were natural accompaniments and by the mid-nineteenth century coffee- and tea-time were established as meals in their own right among all classes of society, throughout Europe and even in America, where the immigrants from Europe had taken their customs.

Today the different European and American baking traditions still reflect their historical roots. Italian regional baking in the South, in Sicily and Sardinia bears a strong resemblance to the early eastern influences, and is often inclined to be over-sweet and rather heavy. Elsewhere in Italy, although the traces still remain of early introductions, more anonymous cream-filled confections of north European origins now fill the shelves of the Italian *pasticceria*, and the housewife very rarely bakes at home.

In Hungary and Austria, Switzerland and Germany, the home-baking tradition of the housewife is still deeply rooted — her reputation as a homemaker is important to her; how better to show this off than with a heavily laden coffee table? In France the tradition of the *pâtissier* — the specialist pastry cook — continues and it is customary to buy cakes from him. Home baking in France tends to confine itself to fruit tarts, but even this custom is becoming less common.

In Britain the plainer fare and Christmas cakes are still baked at home; but the temptations of ready-made cream-filled pastries are strong. America has long fallen prey to the 'take-away' mood and has accepted a poor replacement for what was once good-quality baked produce.

More recently, however, while the tea- and coffee-time traditions are still popular in Europe and America, the last decade has seen a further development in the consumption of sweet confectionery. The dinner table once again offers a place for the special dessert — a gâteau or a torte of European splendor — at the end of an elegant meal.

This book is a celebration of the diversity and sometimes lavish richness of traditional bakery in Europe and America. It is planned as a working manual and inspiration, for both beginners and experienced cooks. Basic recipes and step-by-step techniques are given at the back of the book; general hints and techniques such as the selection of basic ingredients and the use of the oven, lie at the front. Please study these sections carefully.

Barbara Maher

Weights and measures
The metric system is the most accurate. Measurements throughout the book are given in metric and American cups. It is important to use either all metric, or all cups, never a mixture.

Hints and Techniques

A few basic rules apply to baking, which, when observed, remove many of the uncertainties and help avoid possible mistakes.

First, read the recipe from start to finish. Then, make sure that all the ingredients are available; do not try to substitute any or adjust the quantities, rather choose another recipe.

Next, assemble all the ingredients and, if possible, leave them in the kitchen for about an hour to reach the same temperature. Prepare the utensils; grease and line the baking pans; weigh out all the ingredients accurately, sifting, grinding, grating or chopping as necessary. Everything should be ready when baking commences.

Switch on the oven to preheat it; all cakes must be baked in an oven heated to the correct temperature.

Stocking the pantry

Keep your store cupboard stocked with the basic ingredients so that you may bake whenever the fancy takes you, but make sure you do not over-buy: everything should be quite fresh.

Eggs

Almost every cake contains eggs and the fresher they are the better. They give flavor, color and texture, and, when the whites are beaten separately, the snow adds lightness and air to the mixture and may be the only leavening agent.

The recipes in the book all use large eggs. Each egg weighs approximately 50g/2oz and the white weighs about 30g/1oz.

To separate an egg, crack it sharply on the edge of a small bowl and break the shell in two; lightly transfer the yolk from one half of the shell to the other, letting the white albumen drop through into the bowl beneath. Place the yolk in another bowl. Should any yolk get caught in the whites, scoop it out carefully using the jagged edge of the shell, because any trace left behind will inhibit the whites from beating to their greatest volume. Left-over whites may be stored in an air-tight jar in the refrigerator for 8-10 days; they may also be frozen in ice-cube trays and kept for up to 6 months. Bring them to room temperature before using them.

Butter

Only butter should be used for baking as the fine flavor is an essential ingredient to the taste of the cake. Use a good quality, slightly salted or unsalted butter for general baking, but unsalted butter is better for the more delicate flavor of cake fillings.

Flour

All-purpose is used in most recipes, and baking powder may be added to increase the leavening.

Bread or hard wheat flour is better for pastries such as puff and choux that need to stretch and expand well and for yeast dough.

Potato flour or *farina*, which is used in some cakes, has a light, powdery but dense texture, and a sweet and nutty taste.

Cornstarch may be used, but it has little flavor.

Always weigh flour before sifting and always sift flour before using. Hold a fine-mesh sieve or flour sifter high in the air and gently shake the flour through it into a bowl or on to a sheet of paper. Repeat three or four times so that the flour is well aerated, and if baking powder is used, sift it together with the flour.

Sugar

Granulated sugar is used in most recipes as well as for boiling and making syrups; make sure that it is free of lumps and sift it if necessary.

Confectioners' sugar must always be sifted. It is often used in fillings since it is not as sweet as granulated sugar and, mixed with water and flavorings, makes a simple icing. Dredge it over a cake as a simple decoration.

Brown or *muscavado sugars* tend to become hard and lumpy. Never use them in this state, but soften them again by putting them in a bowl and laying a damp cloth over and leaving overnight, or warming the sugar gently in a low oven for a few moments.

Syrup, molasses and honey

To weigh syrup, molasses or honey warm the container in a pan of hot water so that the contents run more easily. Oil the measuring cup or spoon so the thick liquid will slip off easily, or measure the butter, lard or shortning first, then measure the syrup, molasses or honey in the same cup or spoon.

Golden syrup is pale yellow and thick, with a honey-like consistency, but its taste is unique and very much a part of British sweet cookery.

Chocolate

Bittersweet or *bitter chocolate* has the best flavor for baking. Choose only the finest dessert varieties or European cooking chocolate, and avoid the cheaper cooking varieties found on many supermarket shelves.

Use *cocoa powder* only when indicated — never substitute cocoa for chocolate.

Do not melt chocolate directly over heat as it burns very quickly. Break it up and place the pieces in a small bowl or on a plate set over a pan, a quarter filled with gently simmering water, so that the chocolate does not get too hot. Leave it to melt without stirring. Use as directed in the recipes.

Chocolate curls   To make simple curls the chocolate should be at room temperature; shave off long slivers using a vegetable peeler.

For a more professional look, melt the chocolate in a bowl set over simmering water, let it cool for one minute, then pour it on to a lightly oiled work-top and spread it out with a metal spatula to $\frac{1}{8}$in. Leave to cool and, when it is on the point of setting, hold a long sharp knife upright, with a hand at either end, and pull it towards you with a gentle sawing action. Lay the curls on a baking sheet to harden. Store between sheets of wax paper in an air-tight container.

Nuts

Nuts are an important feature in European baking, often taking the place of flour and, when blended with eggs and sugar, make light cakes with a distinctive flavor. Almonds, hazelnuts and walnuts are most common, while pistachios and pine nuts suggest a Middle Eastern influence; pecan nuts are popular in the United States although almost unheard of in Europe.

The keeping qualities of nuts depends on the amount of oil in them. Walnuts are particularly susceptible to rancidity.

Always check that nuts are fresh before you buy them — they are usually date marked. If possible, buy whole, shelled nuts and grind them as they are needed; ready-ground nuts are inclined to be too powdery and rather tasteless, although split and flaked varieties generally have a good flavor.

To blanch almonds and pistachios plunge the nuts into boiling water and boil for 2 minutes. Take the pan off the heat, drain a few almonds at a time and rub each between the fingers and thumb to pop off the skins. Lay the nuts on a baking sheet and dry them in a cool oven (275°F) for about one hour.

Raw, ground almonds are used in some recipes, and they give a pleasant, chewy texture to a cake. Rub the brown skins with a clean towel to remove any dust before grinding. Use a food processor or liquidizer to grind the nuts or pound them in a mortar.

Take care not to over-grind nuts as this releases their natural oils, making them gritty and moist and tainting the taste. It helps to add a little sugar or egg white taken from the main recipe, or rose or orange-flower water, as you work.

To skin hazelnuts, which are usually roasted to bring out their full flavor, spread the shelled nuts on a baking tray and leave for about 10 minutes in a preheated (350°F) oven . As soon as the hazelnuts start to brown and the skins split and flake, lift the tray from the oven. Roll a few nuts at a time in a coarse cloth to remove the cases, shake off the loose skins and brown the nuts for a little longer until golden. Leave to cool. Grind or chop as for almonds.

To caramelize hazelnuts gently melt a little granulated sugar in a frying pan and cook until it turns a very pale golden color. Take the pan off the heat and quickly drop in whole, toasted hazelnuts and stir around briskly with a wooden spoon until they are well coated with the caramel. Lay to set on a sheet of wax paper or an oiled baking sheet.

Walnuts do not need skinning, but extra care must be taken when grinding them as their oils are particularly bitter; blend with the sugar, egg or perfumed water as for almonds.

Chestnuts 1lb *fresh chestnuts* will yield about 12oz peeled nuts. Boil the nuts in salted water for 15-20 minutes until the skins and inner casings may be easily peeled away. Boil the peeled nuts in fresh water until soft. Drain well and sieve.

Dehydrated chestnuts do not have as good a flavor, but they come ready shelled. Boil them in salted water for 45-50 minutes, drain and sieve. $4\frac{1}{2}$oz dried chestnuts will yield 9oz reconstituted nuts.

Lemon and orange zests and peels

Zest is the grated, oily rind of the fruits. Take

care not to grate the white pith beneath the skin as it has a bitter, unpleasant taste. Grate the peel on a fine-textured grater or use a metal zester tool, which consists of a row of tiny holes that cut and curl fine, long slivers of peel.

Vanilla bean and vanilla essence

Fresh vanilla bean has a distinctive, pleasant aroma and is used extensively in European baking. For a more concentrated fragrance, split about a quarter of the pod in half lengthways, scoop out the tiny black grains and blend them with the cake mixture. For a gentler aroma, *vanilla-flavored sugar* is more suitable. Plunge a whole pod cut into pieces or the scraped out left-over pods into a close-stoppered jar filled with sugar. Top up the jar with more sugar as it is used; the pod will keep fresh for up to a year.

Buy pure *vanilla extract* only from health-food stores or delicatessen shops; the synthetic varieties are over-strong and have an unpleasantly sharp flavor.

Old European recipes generally used a small proportion of whole *bitter almonds*, but these are no longer available. The extract is very concentrated, and a drop or two improves the flavour in almond cakes. Buy it in delicatessen and health-food shops.

Orange-flower water and rose water

These perfumed essences originated in early Middle Eastern cuisine and were brought to the west by the Crusaders. Use a very small measure, for their aromas are so powerful that they quickly overwhelm and dominate other flavors.

Spices

Whole, freshly ground spices have a more pungent fragrance and stronger flavor than ready-ground varieties. Grind them in a mortar or coffee mill as they are needed.

Dried and crystallized fruits

Golden raisins, raisins and currants are the most familiar dried fruits used in baking, but dried pears and apples are also popular in European tea-breads. You may like to substitute apricots, which add an unusual nutty taste, or prunes, with their rich color and added moisture. Preserved ginger gives a sharp tang, and crystallized pineapple a sweet chewiness.

Choose dried fruits that are plump and

1. *Copper egg white bowl*
2. *Gupelhupf mould*
3. *American measuring spoons*
4. *Plastic spatula or scraper*
5. *Nylon mesh sieve*
6. *Metal spatula*
7. *Large metal spoon for folding in*
8. *Large cake slice or spatula*
9. *Balloon whisk*
10. *Sugar thermometer*
11. *Guttered mold or Rehrücken pan*
12. *Wire cooling racks*
13. *Deep tartlet pans or bun pans*
14. *Jelly roll pan*
15. *Angelfood cake pan*
16. *Madeleine pans*
17. *Deep, loose-bottomed cake pan*
18. *Fluted tart pan with loose base*
19. *Loaf pan*
20. *Spring-form pans*
21. *American measuring cups*
22. *Patterned ring or savarin mold*
23. *Unlined copper sugar boiler*
24. *Cookie cutters*
25. *Plain rolling pin*
26. *Pastry brush*

moist looking; avoid old fruit that is shrivelled and hard as it will not change, even during baking.

Steep raisins and currants in water for about ½ hour, then dry on a baking sheet in a medium oven for 5 minutes. Plump golden raisins in a little brandy or dark rum to give added flavor. Apricots and prunes should be soaked in water for a short time, but pears and apples need longer, 3-4 hours.

Crystallized cherries, orange and lemon peel, angelica, pineapple and ginger should all be moist and glistening with sugar; hardened fruit will have lost its texture and fine taste.

Dried and crystallized fruits tend to sink to the bottom of a cake mixture as the cake bakes. To help prevent this, dry the fruit very carefully, then coat it thoroughly with a mixture of 1-2 tbsp of flour taken from the main quantity and ½ tsp of baking powder.

Soft cheeses

Curds cheese is the most suitable soft cheese for baking and does not need sieving. It contains about 12 per cent butter fat and has a good, but not too rich, flavor with a dry texture. If it is difficult to obtain, use a mixture of half cottage cheese and half cream cheese, but drain both well before sieving.

Ricotta cheese also has a low fat content, and its sweet nutty taste is quite distinctive; but make quite sure that it is absolutely fresh.

Gelatine

See individual recipes for quantities, but the basic method is to pour very hot, but not boiling, water into a cup. Sprinkle over the gelatine powder and stir to dissolve. Leave for about 10 minutes; if it has not dissolved completely, place the cup in a pan of warm water and heat gently, stirring all the time, until the lumps have disappeared and the liquid is clear. Leave to cool, then beat and fold it into the mixture as instructed.

Oven

Oven temperatures

The temperatures indicated for each recipe are for regular ovens, where the heat source lies on either side, or at the top or the bottom, of the oven. Fan-assisted and fan ovens work on a different principle, and the heat is circulated by a fan, which gives the same temperature throughout the oven. Because there is little variance in heat, cakes are inclined to bake more

quickly and to dry out. It may be necessary, therefore, to reduce the oven temperature by between 25° and 50° in every 200°F, but please consult the literature accompanying your appliance for precise directions.

Oven thermometer

An accurate oven is essential for successful baking. It should be well insulated and draft-proof, as a discrepancy of a few degrees in the temperature can have a disastrous effect. Regular checking with an oven thermometer helps avoid this.

Baking and testing

Cakes must always be baked in a preheated oven. Never open the oven door before at least three-quarters of the cooking time has elapsed, otherwise the delicate structure may collapse.

A cooked cake should have risen well, be slightly domed in the middle and have a golden color; it should be shrinking very slightly from the sides of the pan.

To test for readiness, lightly press a finger on the center of the cake, which should feel quite firm and springy. If the impression of the fingerprint remains, bake the cake for a few minutes more. You may also test by inserting a skewer or wooden toothpick in the center of the cake and withdrawing it gently; it should be dry and clean. If any mixture still adheres, the cake needs further cooking.

Cooling cakes

A cake must always be cooled on a wire rack, so that the air may circulate around it; this stops the cake getting soggy in the middle and collapsing. Cheesecakes are prone to collapse and crack as they cool, but the flavor and texture remain unaffected. This is part of their appeal!

Storing cakes

Store cakes in a cool place in an air-tight container or wrapped in aluminum foil or plastic wrap. Filled cream cakes should be covered and stored in the refrigerator or frozen as applicable; please see the individual instructions.

Freezing

Some cakes may be frozen quite successfully and details are given where appropriate. Cooled cakes should be frozen open on a tray before being close-wrapped and stored, but cakes made with fresh yeast should be wrapped and frozen while still warm to retain maximum freshness.

FRANCE

Pâte à Choux   Cream Puffs   Profiteroles
Gâteau Pithiviers   Millefeuilles
Millefeuilles with Raspberries or Strawberries and Whipped Cream
Tarte Normande aux Pommes   Flans aux Fruits
Raspberry, Strawberry, or Redcurrant Flan   Fruit Tartlets
Roulades   Bûche de Noël   Mocha Gâteau
Orange Mousseline Gâteau   Gâteau des Rois   Le Succès
Madeleines

Bread is an important staple of the French diet. It appears at every meal and is also used quite extensively in cooking. The familiar long sticks — baguettes — of white crusty bread come in various lengths and thicknesses and are freshly baked twice and sometimes even three times a day.

Every country has regional specialities and traditions in bakery, but it is France that has had the greatest influence on the pâtisserie of Europe and America today.

Pies and tarts were among the earliest pastries in the French pastrycook's repertoire, as they could be baked on the hearth without an oven. The crusts were made with fine wheat flour, probably with lard and water, and they usually contained a savory filling, fruit fillings being quite exceptional. Most pies were baked with a lid of pastry and then tinted with saffron or 'gilded' with egg yolks, a practice still common well into the nineteenth century.

The 1650s saw the publication of two important culinary works, which influenced French cooking and baking for a considerable time. *Le Cuisinier François*, by François Pierre de la Varenne, appeared in 1651 and the second work, *Le Pâtissier François*, also reputed to be his, appeared three years later. In these books we find all the basic flour recipes: shortcrust pastry, raised pie pastry, *pâte feuilletée* and puff and choux pastes made with oil. Choux paste had appeared earlier in the century, and although nineteenth-century historians believed that Claude Lorraine, the seventeenth century landscape painter, was the inventor of puff pastry, the Bishop of Amiens had mentioned it as early as 1311. Its composition is reminiscent of Near Eastern fila pastry, which suggests even earlier origins. La Varenne also includes delicately spiced, beaten egg and sugar batters, the types of sponges from which sweet cakes later developed.

There are waffles, darioles and talmouses (cheese tarts), baked choux buns, beignets and fritters, and a confection like today's Italian meringue, made with beaten egg whites and sugar syrup. There are macaroons and marzipan, and a macaroon base made with almonds, egg whites and sugar, similar to *succès* (p. 33). La Varenne also includes two yeasted, brioche-type pastries made with eggs and butter. A sugar icing appears as do fillings of *crème pâtissière* and *frangipane* made with almonds, together with a preparation of mixed spices for flavoring the cream fillings.

The book was apparently inspired by an Italian work published in Venice almost a century earlier. It mentions a typical tart, filled with pastry cream, flavored with cinnamon and rose-flower water, Corinth raisins, pinenuts and candied lemon zest — all strong influences of Islamic cuisine. The top is covered with a pastry trellis, and there are instructions for baking, whether in an oven or in a covered skillet buried in hot coals. Many such tarts are finished with a dusting of sugar, which is glazed in the oven for a little longer, then finished with a few splashes of rose water. They must have been extremely sweet.

There are also the fruit *tourtes*, still much loved in France. La Varenne lists redcurrants, cherries, apricots, plums, gourds, pumpkins and melons, apples, pears and fruit conserves — all covered with a pastry lid. Open-faced tarts and flans appear too, but only with cheese fillings.

Some sixty years later, cookery books show a great increase in the quantity of sweet flavorings and emphasize skill and delicacy in baking. New flavors — chocolate and coffee — are introduced, and sponge batter mixtures proliferate as the use of egg whites, meringue and macaroons increases.

About this time a slow change in the styles of French cuisine began. There was a gradual refinement as the educated classes became aware of their diet, and the dining element, of court ceremonies, increased in importance. The culture of Paris and of the court of Louis XIV, the 'Sun King' was emulated by much of aristocratic Europe, which adopted the cooking styles of the French as well as their language.

The way the aristocracy ate, the presentation and the food itself began to differ from that of the middle classes, the *bourgeoisie*. Table decorations for the élite became important. There were pyramids of foods and fruits and elaborate arrangements depicting landscapes and architectural features made with biscuit doughs, sugar paste and wax. Cardboard cut-outs were used, with colored sugars (commonly known as sand) and trimmings of silk chenille.

In the early nineteenth century there was a revolution in the kitchen when, Antonin Carême, having completed his apprenticeship as a pâtissier, began what was probably the most prestigious and distinguished career in the history of cookery. At the time a pastrycook, who was considered to be as important as a *cuisinier*, was responsible for the architectural *pièces montées*, the grand centerpieces seen on the aristocratic tables. It was in this milieu that Carême worked, in the most distinguished kitchens of Europe. His first two volumes on pâtisserie, published in 1815, were lavishly illustrated. He associated confectionery with architecture, and in his instructions to aspirants he suggested that a close study be made of engravings of classical material — pavilions, temples, ruins, fountains, sculptures, as well as any other relevant subjects — and that detailed scale drawings should be made. But this was only one aspect of his abilities: his recipes for cakes and pastries showed an innovative and original taste that remains unchallenged today. Later Carême turned his attention to the other areas of the kitchen, seeing there further scope for his talents.

At this time the political unrest that was sweeping through France forced a more restrained approach in the kitchens as there was a considerable reduction in the availability of provisions. Carême was well able to cope with the new challenge. Simplifying the more lavish cooking techniques of the old and combining them with the plainer bourgeois style, there evolved *haute cuisine* as we know it today. Despite the huge demands placed on him in the kitchen, he still found time to write several further works on both pâtisserie and *haute cuisine*, which still have their influence today, while his innovations in the pastry kitchen lasted well into this century.

Urbain Dubois, a disciple of Carême's who worked in France towards the end of the nineteenth century, emulated much of the master's work but in a less flamboyant manner. The architectural themes in some *pièces montées* remained, though in a diminished form, and he later introduced many smaller structures depicting more mundane, though rather unusual, everyday subjects, such as an open book with a silk bookmark, a pineapple or a drum, complete with sticks. Interestingly, Dubois tended to use mostly edible materials for the smaller confections, as well as tiny cakes and pastries for additional decoration.

At around this time a new trend in confectionery occurred, layered and cream-filled cakes began to appear, and the piping equipment for cake decoration improved. The technique became far simpler and less time-consuming and well within the capabilities of the less experienced cook.

Petits fours now became popular, though la Varenne had actually mentioned the 'little ovens' of their derivation some 300 years earlier. The basic doughs of sponge and buttery genoese, macaroon, meringue, choux paste, puff and shortcrust pastries offered themselves in miniature, to be filled and iced in a multitude of shapes and

sizes. In his book *The Magic Mountain*, Thomas Mann describes them as 'toothsome, cone-shaped with dainties in lace frills, covered with coloured frosting and filled with chocolate and pistache cream.' These were the new temptations to be admired in the confectioner's windows.

The regional and bourgeois specialities and symbolic festive cakes remain an important element in France's confectionery traditions, but the too exotic and over-decorated extravagances of Carême's time have been abandoned — *croquembouche* (the choux pastry tower) is the sole survivor of his fruited pyramids, and *hérisson*, the chocolate covered sponge roll spiked with almonds, is a poor reminder of Dubois' decorative zeal. However, the best features have been retained to combine cleverly with la Varenne's basic preparations.

A typical display of confectionery in a pâtissier's window: sweet Gugelhupf and brioche breads, gâteau St Honoré and Paris Brest made of choux pastry and various fruit 'tourtes' and flans of which the French are so fond.

'Between four and five o'clock, at the pâtissier's'. Ask a child: he will say that small cakes encourage friendship!

Pâte à Choux

CHOUX PASTRY

130g/1 cup bread flour, sifted
2 tsp sugar
125ml/¹/₂ cup water
125ml/¹/₂ cup milk
100g/7 tbsp lightly salted butter,
  cut small
4 eggs
1 tsp brandy, rum or orange-
  flower water (optional)

400°F for 20 minutes

Makes 22 buns

Choux pastry is thought to have originated in the mid-sixteenth century, and it was especially popular made in deep-fried fritter or beignet form. Today we know it in many different guises, although mainly baked: as small pastries such as éclairs, cream puffs or buns, salambôs, pets de nonne, copenhagens, fabiola or léopolds; larger gâteaux such as St Honoré, religieuse and Paris Brest; and, of course, Croquembouche, the spectacular decorated French wedding-cake, built of small buns in pyramid form and covered with a plume of spun sugar.

The preparation of choux pastry takes very little time and is quite unlike any other baking technique; both the visual reward and the flavor are unusually gratifying. The basic ingredients of butter, flour and water are cooked together to make a type of white sauce, or roux, before the eggs are beaten in. During baking the paste expands and puffs into a crisp hollow shell, almost three times its original size.

Uncooked choux pastry freezes very well for up to 2 months. For small buns pipe or spoon the mixture on to wax paper and open-freeze before packing in air-tight bags. Bake from the freezer 5 minutes longer than the normal time.

Sift the flour and sugar two or three times, finally on to a sheet of wax paper. Set aside. Measure the water and milk into a deep pan, and drop in the butter pieces. Set the pan over heat and warm gently until all the butter has melted, then raise the temperature and bring the liquid to a rolling boil. Draw the pan aside and shoot in the flour mixture all at once. Beat vigorously with a wooden spoon and quickly replace the pan over low heat. Continue beating and cook the paste for just a few seconds more so that the flour is properly combined. The paste should have an ungrained, smooth appearance and roll cleanly off the bottom and sides of the pan into a ball (a floury film is left on the base of the pan). Avoid over-cooking the paste or the finished buns will be heavy. Leave to cool for about 5 minutes.

The mixture may now be beaten in the bowl of an electric mixer as the eggs are added. Care must be taken here as too much egg can spoil the paste, making it too runny, so add a little at a time.

Lightly whisk the eggs together in a separate bowl, and pour about a quarter on to the flour paste, beat vigorously until well combined; add more egg and beat again. Continue adding egg and beating, until the paste is quite firm but elastic — it will drop from a spoon reluctantly when jerked slightly. You may not need quite all of the egg, although if the weather conditions are dry, you may need a little more. Beat the paste well until it is shiny and smooth; finally add the brandy, rum or flower water.

The paste is now ready for use and may be kept for an hour or two if covered with a damp cloth.

Choux pastry must be cooked until all the surfaces are completely browned, otherwise it will collapse and go soggy as it cools. It is, however, inclined to burn rather easily underneath and needs additional protection in the oven. Either use a second large baking sheet, warmed in the oven beforehand, or line the one that you are using with a thick layer of aluminum foil.

To bake choux pastry buns hold a large, flat baking sheet under cold running water for a few seconds to chill it; shake off the excess water but leave it damp. Place teaspoonfuls of the mixture, about 1in high and 2in apart on the baking sheet. Remember that they expand to two or three times their size during baking. Lightly brush a little beaten egg on each one and scatter over a pinch of granulated sugar to give sparkle; chopped or flaked almonds are also nice. Bake in the pre-heated oven.

Choux buns take about 20 minutes to cook. Never open the oven door until at least 15 minutes have elapsed, as the delicate structure will collapse immediately if it is not cooked sufficiently.

The baked pastries will be light, hollow and golden brown. Lift the tray out of the oven and transfer the buns to a wire rack. Pierce each one with a skewer or knife to release the steam inside and leave them to cool.

Choux pastries are best eaten on the day they are baked, but they can be stored for a day or two in an air-tight container, then re-heated in a low oven for about 10 minutes to crisp them up again. They should be filled no more than 1 hour before being served.

Cream Puffs

1 portion choux buns as above
1 cup heavy or
   whipping cream, whipped
3 tbsp vanilla sugar
confectioners' sugar for
   dredging

Flavourings (optional)
1 tbsp Cointreau or Grand
   Marnier or
3 tbsp chopped pistachios or
4 tbsp almond praline
   (p. 101)

Fold the sugar and flavoring into the whipped cream. Slice each bun open enough to press a spoonful of filling into it. Dredge generously with confectioners' sugar to serve.

Crème pâtissière (p. 150) also makes a delicious filling. Flavor it with any of the above or with chocolate or coffee, and cover the top with a little icing of the same flavor.

Profiteroles

Chocolate sauce
250g/9oz dark dessert
   chocolate
1 cup milk
2in vanilla pod, split
2 tbsp heavy cream
40g/3 tbsp butter
50g/¼ cup sugar

Cream-filled puffs (see previous recipe) are served with chocolate sauce as an after-dinner dessert. Pile them on an attractive dish and pipe a few rosettes of whipped cream as decoration. Dredge with confectioners' sugar. Serve the sauce separately or pour a little cold sauce over the profiteroles just before serving. Scatter toasted chopped hazelnuts and pistachios to decorate.

Break the chocolate into small pieces and gently melt them in a bowl that fits snugly over a pan of simmering water. The water must not touch the bowl. In another pan heat the milk with the vanilla pod to boiling point and add the cream; bring it back to a boil and lift the pan off the heat. Remove the vanilla pod and stir in the melted chocolate, butter and sugar. Return the pan to the heat and boil for a few seconds longer so that the sauce blends well. Pour it into a warmed glass jug and use hot or leave to cool.

PROFITEROLES: *Unfilled choux pastry buns also taste good with a coating of caramel. Dip them in lightly colored caramel sugar (p.151) and stud with a few chopped almonds or pistachios. Fill with cream when cooled.*

Millefeuilles

500g/1lb puff pastry (p. 148)
chilled (or use ready-made
fresh or frozen pastry)

425°F for 20 minutes

One thousand leaves is the literal translation, and it is almost true! For by the time the puff paste has been rolled, folded and turned half a dozen times, there are more than 700 layers of trapped air and butter dough. This feather-like assemblage needs only the simplest embellishment, and it makes a sumptuous and impressive after-dinner dessert.

Roll out the pastry on a chilled, floured surface to 1/8in thick, and use a sharp knife to cut it into three equal rectangles, 7 × 12in. Leave to chill for at least 1 hour, or overnight if possible.

Heat the oven. Chill a baking sheet under running cold water and shake off the excess moisture. Transfer one of the pastries to the wet tray, prick all over with a fork to prevent it from puffing too much and bake it in the hot oven until well puffed and golden. Cool on a wire rack. Prepare and bake the other pastries in the same way.

The uncooked, prepared pastry rectangles may be frozen for up to 2 months. Bake from frozen and allow 5 minutes more baking time.

Millefeuilles with Raspberries or Strawberries

400ml/2 cups heavy or
whipping cream
4 tbsp vanilla sugar
2 tbsp kirsch or Grand Marnier
3 rectangles, cooked puff pastry
500g/1lb fresh raspberries or
strawberries, cleaned but
not washed
confectioners' sugar for
dredging

Whisk the cream into soft peaks; lightly beat in the sugar and liqueur.

Smooth half the whipped cream on to a puff pastry rectangle. Cover with a second layer of pastry and spread over the rest of the cream. Reserve one perfect fruit for decoration, and embed the rest in the cream. Lay the last pastry rectangle on top. Dredge the top heavily with sifted confectioners' sugar. Heat a long metal skewer and quickly burn a trellis pattern into the sugar, reheating the skewer as necessary. Place the reserved fruit in the center as decoration and serve on an elegant platter.

This confection may be further enriched by substituting the bottom layer of cream with one of crème pâtissière (p. 150), using half the quantity. Use the remaining whipped cream to pipe rosettes on the top of the cake.

Gâteau Pithiviers

500g/1lb puff pastry (p.148) or
    ready-made fresh or frozen
    pastry, defrosted
1 egg, lightly beaten
confectioners' sugar for
    sprinkling

Almond Paste
65g/²/₃ cup ground almonds
65g/5 tbsp sugar
50g/2oz butter, softened
1 egg yolk
2 tbsp dark rum

450°F for 15 minutes
    then reduce the
    temperature to 400°F for
    30-40 minutes

Pithiviers is a small town, some 80 kilometres south of Paris, which has gained world reknown for the delicious pastry named after it. It is not certain when the cake originated there, but early in the nineteenth century, Antonin Câreme, the famous and influential French chef and pastry-cook, included several variations for the filling in his writings.

The cake is made of a casing of puff pastry that envelopes a delectable rum-flavored almond paste.

The gâteau is at its best eaten lukewarm or only just cooled and, though it takes some time to prepare, it may be frozen assembled, but undecorated and uncooked, for up to 2 months. Defrost for about 30 minutes until a knife will cut into the pastry, before decorating and baking. Allow about 10 minutes more on the basic cooking time.

I recommend this gâteau as dessert for a very special occasion.

The almond paste filling should be chilled and firm before it is used; make it a day ahead if possible.

First make the almond paste. Mix together the ground almonds and sugar and beat to a smooth paste with the butter and egg yolk. Beat in the rum. Cover and leave to chill and harden.

Reserve two-thirds of the puff pastry, wrap in plastic wrap and leave in the refrigerator. Roll the remainder on a floured board, into a 8in circle. Trim the edge cleanly with a sharp knife. Run cold water over a large, flat baking sheet to moisten it and shake off the excess. Transfer the pastry circle to it, cover and chill for 30 minutes.

Smooth the hardened lump of almond paste over the pastry to within 1in of the edge, and lightly brush water on the border. Roll out the remainder of the pastry to twice the thickness of the base, and trim the edges cleanly, as before. Carefully fold the pastry circle over the rolling pin and lay it on top of the almond filling. Press all round the edge firmly to seal the two layers together. Using a sharp, pointed knife dipped in hot water, cut a scalloped border. Cover and chill for 30 minutes.

Brush all over the pastry top with beaten egg, cut a hole in the center and insert a small, buttered aluminum foil chimney in it. Brush a second coat of egg glaze all over.

The decoration is distinctive and traditional. Using a pointed knife, cut into the pastry about ⅛in deep. Inscribe lines radiating from the middle to the scalloped edge in a curved half-moon shape. Prick right through the pastry to the baking sheet in about six places. Bake in the preheated oven for 15 minutes, then reduce the temperature and continue baking. About 10 minutes before the cooking time is complete, sprinkle the top of the cake generously with sifted confectioners' sugar and return the cake to the oven for it to caramelize. The cooked cake should have puffed right up into a dome and be golden in color. Lift out of the oven, remove the foil chimney and leave to cool on the baking sheet set on a wire rack.

GÂTEAU PITHIVIERS: *This puff pastry confection filled with almond paste is quite delicious while still warm.*

STRAWBERRY MILLEFEUILLES: *The buttery, crisp and flaky layers of home-made puff pastry have a much finer flavor than shop-bought varieties. If you take the time, you will be well rewarded by your visitors' compliments.*

MOCHA GÂTEAU: *A richly flavored sponge cake filled with coffee cream.*

Orange Mousseline Gâteau

140g/1 cup plus 1 tbsp
    confectioners' sugar, sifted,
    plus extra for dusting
1 tbsp orange zest
6 egg yolks
55g/½ cup all-purpose flour,
    plus extra for dusting
55g/⅓ cup potato flour
3 egg whites
3 tbsp Grand Marnier or Curaço
butter for greasing
orange fondant icing (p. 154)
candied orange peel for decoration

325°F for 40 minutes

This sponge, known as *biscuit de savoie*, has a light, airy texture. The method of beating egg whites separately before folding them into the main mixture helps give air, and the potato flour gives a fine nutty flavor. These 'biscuit' batter cakes originated in France during the 1600s and by the end of the century there were as many as 24 different recipes.

Beat the sifted sugar and orange zest with the egg yolks until light and foamy. Sift together the two flours to aerate them well. Beat the egg whites in a separate bowl until they stand in firm peaks. Alternately fold in the egg whites and sift the flours into the yolk mixture in three separate stages. Fold in 2 tbsp of the liqueur. Grease and line an 8½in springform pan with wax paper. Butter, then dust the paper with sugar and flour, pour in cake mixture and bake.

When the cake has risen well and is springy to the touch, place on a wire rack to cool.

Take 225g/½lb fondant icing and flavor with the rest of the liqueur and prepare as instructed on p. 154.

Decorate with candied orange peel while still soft. Leave to set overnight before cutting.

Roulades

SPONGE ROLLS

A roulade is a sponge mixture, quickly baked in a shallow rectangular cake tin and rolled around a filling.

Line a jelly roll pan (10 × 14in) with wax paper or aluminum foil, leaving a 1-1½in to hang over on each side and at both ends. Grease well with unsalted butter. Prepare a half portion of genoese or fat-free sponge mixture (pp. 142-5), and pour it straight into the jelly roll pan. Level out lightly. Bake immediately in the preheated oven (450F) for about 10 minutes, until well-risen and golden brown. It will start to shrink away slightly from the edges of the pan.

Meanwhile cover a clean dish cloth with a large sheet of wax paper and dredge liberally with sugar. Turn the cooked sponge straight over on to the sugared paper and carefully peel off the baking paper.

Trim away the crisp edges of sponge on the shorter sides and quickly roll up the pastry from the short side, around the paper, using the dish cloth to help. Lay on a wire rack with the seam underneath and cover with a slightly damp cloth. Leave to cool.

A basic sponge roll can be presented in a number of ways. Bûche de Noël is rather elaborate as befits a celebratory cake; but when the warm sponge is rolled around a filling of raspberry jam, we have the simple and familiar jelly roll.

A fat-free sponge tastes good filled with fresh strawberries or redcurrants; serve it with whipped cream for a luscious light summer dessert. For a rich and tempting confection, flavor the basic sponge mixture with chocolate or coffee and a dash of rum, make a chestnut cream filling and coat the whole with a glossy covering of rich chocolate.

Bûche de Noël

1 cooked genoese sponge roll
   (see above)
1 portion cooked buttercream
   (p. 150)
100g/3¹/₂oz finest semisweet
   dessert chocolate, melted
   and cooled
1 tbsp instant coffee, dissolved
   in ¹/₂ tsp boiling water
3 tbsp dark rum
50g/3 tbsp apricot jam,
   warmed with 2 tbsp water
   and strained

Meringue mushrooms
1 egg white
55g/¹/₄ cup caster sugar

Decoration
cocoa powder
1 tbsp chopped pistachios
2 tbsp almond flakes
cocoa powder
almond paste or marzipan
   tinted green with food
   coloring

This traditional French Yule log is also made with a roll of sponge cake and seems to be of early twentieth century origin. It is usually filled and piped with a chocolate or mocha flavored buttercream and then decorated to look like a broken tree stump, covered with tiny mushrooms, leaves and moss. Use green-tinted almond paste to fashion holly leaves.

To make the mushrooms prepare a basic meringue mixture (p. 140). With a plain nozzle pipe strips to resemble stalks and different-sized circles for the caps on to wax paper; remember that meringue mixture expands as it bakes. Bake at 300°F for about 15-20 minutes until they are crisp and dry. Peel off the paper carefully and leave to cool on a rack.

Prepare the buttercream. Set aside 4 tbsp cream; combine and flavor the rest with the melted chocolate and coffee liquid.

Unroll the sponge and brush with rum. Spread one-third of the chocolate-flavored buttercream over it and roll it up. Trim one end of the roll straight and cut the other at a sharp angle. Brush all the surfaces with warm apricot jam.

Smooth some of the plain cream over each end of the roll, and lay a few mounds on top of it; these will later resemble branch nodules.

Fit a star nozzle into a large pastry bag and fill with chocolate cream. Pipe uneven lines, close together, along the length of the cake, to give a rough, bark-like effect. Pipe over the mounds as well. Slice an angle off one of the mounds to show the inside. Fit a small piping bag with a narrow plain nozzle, and pipe concentric, chocolate cream circles on the plain cream ends.

Dredge a little cocoa on the meringue caps; stick the stalks to the caps with buttercream. Embed the mushrooms in the log. Strew chopped pistachios and almonds for a moss effect and add one or two holly leaves. Chill for 2-3 hours until the cream is firm, or overnight.

Serve on an elegant serving dish or on a polished plank of wood.

Mocha Gâteau

1 portion genoese sponge
   mixture (p. 145)
1 tbsp instant coffee dissolved
   in ¹/₂ tsp boiling water
1 portion cooked mocha
   flavored buttercream, (p. 150)
110g/1 cup flaked almonds,
   toasted

350°F for 30 minutes

Prepare the genoese sponge; mix the coffee liquid into the egg yolk and sugar mixture. Line a greased 8¹/₂in spring-form pan with wax paper. Grease, pour in the mixture and bake until risen and golden. Cool completely.

Make the mocha buttercream.

Split the cake into three layers. Reserve about half the cream and sandwich the three cake layers together with the remainder. Fit a pastry bag with a small star nozzle and fill with cream. Smooth the remainder of the cream over the top and sides of the cake and press the flaked almonds into the sides. Pipe small mocha buttercream stars close together in symmetrical lines. Decorate with chocolate coffee beans. Chill for a day before serving.

BÛCHE DE NOËL: A
traditional Christmas sponge
roll filled with chocolate
buttercream and decorated
with meringue mushrooms.

NORMANDY APPLE FLAN:
The almond pastry-cream
base, flavored with a dash of
calvados, makes this an
unusual apple tart.

Madeleines

130g/½ cup unsalted butter
1 tbsp honey
100g/⅓ cup sugar
1 tbsp brown sugar
pinch salt
3 eggs
2in vanilla pod, split
130g/1 cup all-purpose flour,
    sifted
flaked almonds

350°F for 25 minutes

Makes 36 cakes

When madeleines are mentioned one immediately thinks of Marcel Proust. In his *Remembrance of Things Past* the French author recalls his childhood and Sunday mornings taking lime tea and madeleines with his Aunt in Combrey. He found 'the taste of the crumb of madeleine soaked in her decoction of lime-flowers ... an exquisite pleasure [that] invaded my senses'.

The plump little sponge cakes are baked in special embossed molds that resemble the 'fluted scallop of a pilgrim's shell' and that give them their characteristic puffed dome. (They may of course be baked in ordinary muffin pans or tins in which case they look like ordinary sponge cakes!)

Serve them in true Proustian style with the French herbal lime tea, *tisane de tilleul*.

Gently melt the butter in the honey and set aside to cool. Beat the granulated and brown sugars with the salt and eggs until the ribbon stage (p. 142). Beat in the vanilla seeds.

Lightly fold in the flour in three stages and finally fold in the cooled butter and honey mixture, taking care not to mix in any of the sediment in the bottom of the pan. Half fill each of the buttered and floured madeleine molds and sprinkle a few flaked almonds on top of each. Bake until risen and golden. Leave to cool on a wire rack before storing in an air-tight container. They should keep fresh for up to a week.

Flans aux Fruits

sweet shortcrust pastry for a
    8½in loose-bottomed tart
    pan or spring-form pan
    (p. 145)
¾-1kg/1½-2lb ripe fruit
lemon juice
3 tbsp apricot jam
3 tbsp confectioners' sugar,
    sifted

375°F for 50-60 minutes

Fruit flans are much loved in France. Laden with glistening apricots, peaches, greengages, mirabelle plums or cherries, they sparkle temptingly to catch the eye. In former times, puff pastry was used as a base, but now sweet shortcrust pastry is preferred as it gives a crisper base. Choose seasonal fruits; they should be unblemished and fully ripe. Most of all be generous with the quantities as the fruit shrinks as it bakes.

Place the flan on a second baking sheet in the oven to add crispness to the base.

Line the base and 1in up the sides of the pan with the pastry. Prick all over with a fork and chill. Wash and dry the fruit carefully; stone cherries and mirabelle plums but leave whole. Cut other fruits in half and remove the stones. Cut peaches into thick slices and rub them with lemon juice to stop them going brown.

Arrange the whole fruits, the fruit halves or slices in circles, cut sides up and each overlapping the preceding one a little; reverse the direction of the fruit for each new circle. Bake in the preheated oven.

Meanwhile, heat the apricot jam with 2 tbsp water until slightly thick; strain.

Remove the flan from the oven and leave in the pan on a wire rack to cool for 10 minutes. Lift off the outer rim of the pan and slide the flan off the base on to the rack. Dust with confectioners' sugar all over, then brush the whole fruited surface with the warm jam, which will cool into a glossy glaze.

Serve when cold with whipped cream on the side.

Raspberry, Strawberry or Redcurrant Flan

Soft fruits must not be baked. Bake blind a pastry shell as above (p. 146). leave to cool.

Shortly before serving fill the flan case with the prepared fruits (500g/1lb) and, if you wish, glaze the surface with 3 tbsp redcurrant jelly warmed with 2 tbsp kirsch. Serve with whipped cream.

You may prefer to half fill the cooked flan with crème pâtissière (p. 150) or crème frangipane (below) before adding the fruit.

Fruit Tartlets
These are made in exactly the same way; the 9½ amount of shortcrust pastry (p. 145) makes 14 deep tartlet cases.

Tarte Normande aux Pommes

NORMANDY APPLE TART

22cm/8½in spring-form pan
  lined with sweet shortcrust
  pastry (p. 145), chilled
500g/1lb crisp, eating apples
  (Red or Golden Delicious)
2 tbsp sugar plus extra for
  dusting
1 tsp cinnamon

Crème frangipane
250ml/1 cup milk
2in vanilla pod, split
3 egg yolks
40g/3 tbsp sugar
40g/4½ tbsp all-purpose flour,
  sifted
pinch salt
1 tbsp unsalted butter, melted
  and browned
1 tbsp ground almonds
1 tbsp calvados or kirsch
2 tbsp apricot jam
100ml/½ cup heavy cream

350°F for 60 minutes

When one thinks of Normandy in culinary terms, butter and cream, apples and calvados spring to mind. What could be better than when they are all combined in this typical apple tart?

Prick the base of the pastry case and par-bake for 15 minutes. Leave to cool (p. 145).

Make the custard. Bring the milk to the boil and infuse with the vanilla pod. Mix together in a pan the egg yolks, sugar, flour and salt; remove the vanilla pod and pour the milk on to the mixture, beating all the time. Place the pan on a low heat and stir continuously until the custard thickens. Pour the custard into a bowl and beat in the brown butter, almonds and calvados. Leave to cool.

Whisk the cream until firm, reserving about three-quarters of it for decoration. Fold the remainder of the cream into the cooled custard and spread it over the par-baked flan; it should be about half full.

Peel, core and quarter the apples and cut them into ¼in slices. Pack the slices tightly together and overlapping on the cream in the flan. Scatter over the sugar and cinnamon and bake in the preheated oven. When the apples have colored and the pastry is shrinking away from the sides of the tin, lift the tart out of the oven and leave to cool in the pan, set on a wire rack. Brush over the apples with warm apricot jam.

Pipe the reserved whipped cream as decoration and dust lightly with sugar just before serving.

GÂTEAU DES ROIS: *It is customary to embed a silver trinket or coin in the dough of this Epiphany cake before it is baked. The person who then finds it in his or her slice is crowned king of the evening.*

FRESH FRUIT TARTS *of strawberries; mirabelle plums; apricots cooked on a base of crème pâtissière gooseberries and black muscat grapes; raspberry and gooseberry tartlets.*

31

Gâteau des Rois

TWELFTH NIGHT CAKE

330g/3 cups bread flour
75g/⅓ cup sugar
110ml/⅓ cup water heated to
　blood heat
15g/1 tbsp fresh yeast
75g/⅓ cup butter, softened
3 eggs
2 tsp grated lemon zest
1 tsp salt
1 dried bean or silver coin
1 egg, slightly beaten
3 tbsp coffee sugar crystals,
　rock or preserving sugar
1 tbsp strained apricot jam
55g/2oz candied angelica,
　lemon and orange peel, cut
　in strips
55g/2oz glacé cherries

375° for 20-30 minutes

Epiphany, which falls on 6 January, is still celebrated in Europe, and was in England until early in the twentieth century.

A traditional twelfth night cake is always baked. In France this varies from region to region. In the northern provinces and around Paris it is a simple galette, a type of tart made of puff pastry and filled with almond paste, rather like Pithiviers (p. 21), while in the south, a yeasted dough similar to 'brioche' baked in the shape of a crown is favoured.

There is a charming custom connected with the Epiphany cake, for each one contains either a small porcelain figure, a silver coin or, in the past, a bean. The intention is that, when the cake is cut, the person whose slice contains the token is crowned king or queen for the night. It then falls to him or her to entertain the guests in their own home and offer in turn, yet another gâteau des rois. In this way the entire month of January becomes a merry extension of the Christmas festivities.

The following recipe comes from the Bordeaux region. The dough is left to rise overnight, so finishing preparation takes less time than is customary with yeast cakes. It does taste best on the day that it is baked, but if you prefer to bake it earlier, it may be frozen while it is still warm.

Make a sponge batter (p. 149) with 65g/⅔ cup flour and 1 tsp sugar taken from the main recipe and the water and yeast. Beat well, cover and set aside to rise. Beat the butter and the rest of the sugar until pale and creamy, beat in the eggs one at a time and the lemon zest. Sift the flour and salt two or three times and finally into a large bowl. Make a well in the middle and drop in the butter mixture. Draw in a little flour from the sides and add the yeast batter. Mix all the ingre-dients thoroughly and beat hard; it should be quite a limp dough but elastic and shiny with large bubbles of air. Cover the bowl with a clean towel and leave it overnight in the cool kitchen or pantry to rise and at least double in bulk.

Next day, turn out the dough on to a floured surface, knock it back and knead in the dried bean or silver coin for a few moments. Pinch off pieces of dough and make six hazelnut-sized balls; set them aside. Cut off two-thirds of the remaining dough and roll it into a rope about 22in long; curve it round into a circle and pinch the ends firmly together. Transfer to a large (10½in), well-buttered baking sheet and carefully brush the top only with beaten egg.

Divide the remaining dough into two and roll each piece into a rope a little longer than the first one. Lightly twist the two together into a braid and carefully lay it in a circle on top of the egg-washed ring. Pinch the ends well to secure them. Brush a dab of egg on the base of each reserved dough ball and space them equally apart on the braided ring. Lightly cover the crown with a floured cloth and leave to rise for 45-60 minutes until risen to about double in bulk. Brush all the surfaces lightly with egg and scatter over the sugar crystals. Bake in the preheated oven until golden brown.

While the cake is still warm, brush the top with strained apricot jam and stick the candied fruits and cherries on the surface to resemble jewels in a crown. Leave to cool.

Serve for Epiphany with a glass of champagne.

Le Succès

Meringue
(p. 140 for preparation
    method)
*260g/2¹/₃ cups ground toasted
    hazelnuts*
270g/1¹/₂ cups sugar
2 tbsp all-purpose flour
6 egg whites
2 tbsp vanilla sugar
*1 portion cooked egg yolk and
    buttercream filling (p. 150)
    flavored with chocolate*
*1 whole toasted hazelnut for
    decoration*

*300°F for approximately 1
    hour*

This exquisite cake is often called Japonais. It is a delicious combination of meringue and nut layers (almonds or hazelnuts), with chocolate or mocha buttercream filling and icing. In France it is baked in a variety of shapes — circular, heart-shaped, rectangular, square or oval — and may be decorated in as simple or lavish a way as befits the occasion. It makes a lovely after-dinner dessert and may be frozen for up to 2 months.

Grind the hazelnuts for this recipe yourself, as the flavor is far better and they should be a little coarse.

Prepare three baking sheets with wax paper. Draw the chosen shape on each.

Mix together 165g/1¹/₃ cups hazelnuts, 140g/²/₃ cup sugar and the flour; set aside. Beat the egg whites in a large, spotlessly clean bowl until they hold firm, snowy peaks. Beat in the rest of the sugar and vanilla sugar until the mixture is firm and glossy. Using a large metal spoon, lightly fold in the nut, sugar and flour mixture. Divide the mixture evenly between the three baking sheets and level out, taking care not to break down the delicate aerated structure. Because of the nut content the succès bases rise little.

Bake them in the preheated oven until lightly colored; they will feel slightly soft to the touch while warm but become crisp and brittle as they cool. Leave on the paper to cool on wire racks.

Prepare the chocolate buttercream filling. (If it has been previously chilled, bring to room temperature for an hour before it is needed.)

To assemble the cake trim the meringue bases to the same size. Place one on a wire rack. Spread one-third of the buttercream over it and cover with the second layer. Smooth over half the remaining cream and place the last meringue on top. Cover the top and sides of the cake with the remaining cream. Press the last of the hazelnuts all around the side of the cake. Place one whole hazelnut in the center. Transfer to a serving dish and chill for at least 3-4 hours or, if possible, overnight.

The top may be piped with a chocolate buttercream decoration if wished.

ORANGE MOUSSELINE
GÂTEAU: *A light and airy,
fondant-covered sponge
cake. Fill it with Grand
Marnier-flavored egg and
buttercream for a grander
occasion.*

LE SUCCÈS: *Nut meringue layers and chocolate butter cream make this a very successful dessert.*

MADELEINES: *Marcel Proust's favorite sponges, to be served with lime tea.*

BRITAIN

Lardy Cake A Light Pound Cake Simnel Cake
Yorkshire Curd Tart Old-fashioned Ginger Snaps
Scottish Shortbread Cornish Saffron Bread Spiced Apple Tart
Plum Cake Lemon Meringue Pie Flapjacks

Traditional baking in Britain is quite different from the ornate splendors of French *pâtisserie* and different again from the rich and luscious confections of the Austro-Hungarian Empire. Cake recipes first appeared in household manuscripts in Britain during the seventeenth century. Before then baking had tended to be rather plain: gingerbread and wafers, pies, hard biscuits and plain breads, which, only in later times, were enriched with eggs and fruit.

Gingerbread and wafers were made by specialist tradesmen who peddled them in the streets and at local fairs. Piemakers used a variety of flour pastes for their coffins (or tarts) and filled them with meat or fish fillings flavored with strange combinations of sweet, savory and spiced ingredients. Cheese tarts were common, and there were others made with egg, dried fruits and spices. By the eighteenth century however, both the quality of the pastry and the choice of fillings had altered and had become much more like those we are familiar with today. Lemon cheese, orange, sorrel, peach, pippin and pineapple were used, and 'umble' pie developed into a rich confection of mincemeat, apple and dried fruit.

Biscuits of the time tended to be on the hard side, although simnels and cracknels, which were boiled before being baked, were of a lighter, biscuity consistency. The biscuit and cake breads of the sixteenth and seventeenth centuries were generally served at banquets and offered to special visitors with a glass of wine. They were usually unleavened, spiced and flavored with seeds, and baked as flat, small cakes in tin, biscuit pans or on metal plates. Yeasted biscuit breads — French biscuit — were always baked twice: first in a long and narrow loaf shape and then cut into slices, sprinkled with sugar and dried out like a rusk. 'Ship's biscuit' is a somewhat unpalatable variety of these. In the eighteenth century wafers were offered with dessert sweetmeats and to accompany jelly, and they were also used as a base for marzipan confections, French macaroons and other almond cakes. By this time the range of biscuits, or cookies, had increased considerably; they were essentially small cakes, of short pastry or a sponge and batter base, flavored exotically with Eastern spices and sometimes even iced.

Breads were enriched with dried fruits and flavored with spices and sometimes caraway seed. They were baked as loaves or small buns, and by the late seventeenth century a buttered slice, together with a cup of chocolate or coffee, one of the new beverages, would serve as a light breakfast. The popularity of fruited doughs grew rapidly, and many regional specialities appeared. Among these were Bath cakes, flavored with caraway comfits, and Banbury cake, with its rich filling of currants, which, like a similar black bun from Scotland, sometimes featured at wedding feasts.

Pikelets were enjoyed by the Midlanders, while the Welsh offered griddle cakes.

Early cakes were generally very large, round or oval and baked only for special occasions. A typical recipe would call for as many as seven or eight pounds of flour, several pounds of dried fruits, numerous eggs and butter, cream and spices, with ale-barm to help raise it. Small cakes were rarely baked, although sometimes spiced varieties would be served as an alternative accompaniment to wafers with wine at a banquet.

A lighter type of cake appeared early in the seventeenth century. The proportion of ingredients, which included many more eggs, and the preparation technique differed from that of the heavier cakes. In the eighteenth century seeds were often substituted for fruits, as they were lighter, while more eggs gave a firmer texture. By the middle of the century, eggs had surplanted yeast as the aerating ingredient in a cake mixture — not unlike the sponge mixtures that were being introduced from France.

In 1780s the first tin hoops were invented and cakes that had previously been laid on buttered papers in the oven were now held in shape and so rose evenly. The size of cakes were reduced although a 'small' cake still used 2 lbs of flour. In the 1860s there was a revolution in the kitchen as more sophisticated cooking ranges with side boilers and ovens for baking were invented. Whereas before only the bread baker had had the facilities to bake larger goods, the possibility was now open to all.

In 1610, a new beverage was brought to Europe from China by the Dutch — tea. Some fifty years later it was introduced to Britain and came to play a significant role in the eating and drinking habits of the land. Until then, coffee had been the favoured drink and chocolate too, was popular, and it was, in fact, in the coffee-houses that tea was first served. Literature was distributed in the coffee-houses giving instructions on the art of blending and making tea in the home. It was very expensive — a pound of the cheapest tea cost about one-third of a skilled worker's weekly wage, which is why lockable tea-caddies came into use.

Despite the cost, by 1750 all classes of people drank tea: 'You have it twice a day and, though the expense is considerable, the humblest peasant has his tea twice a day just like the rich man', wrote the Comte de la Rochefoucauld in 1784. It was fashionable in high society to take a dish of tea at noon, to have an elegant tea-table for afternoon tea, and to make the taking of tea a prolonged after-dinner social occasion.

The tea merchants also brought teapots with them from the East, much to the delight of the British pottery manufacturers who copied the Chinese teasets in both simple and elegant designs. By the middle of the eighteenth century a handsome porcelain tea-service would consist of a teapot and cover, a coffee pot and cover, a sugar bowl, stand and cover, twelve tea bowls or cups and twelve saucers, six coffee cups, a milk jug and cover, a slop-bowl, a spoon tray, a teapot stand and tea cannisters. Large bread-and-butter plates were added a little later, but tea plates were a mid-Victorian addition. Chinese-style tea bowls were in use until the early nineteenth century. A really elegant home would show off its equipage of tea- and coffee-pots in silver, with milk jugs and sugar bowls on a silver tray, on one side the china cups and saucers and on the other a silver-plated kettle on a stand, with a spirit lamp beneath to provide additional hot water.

At the beginning of the nineteenth century, as the gap between luncheon and dinner became longer, the custom of taking afternoon tea started in fashionable circles. Anna, Duchess of Bedford is said to have introduced it, and to assuage 'the pangs of hunger' she offered bread and butter and cakes. At first the light repast usually lasted for little more than an hour, between 4 and 5.30 p.m., but by the middle of the century it had become a more substantial affair. Small, wafer-thin sandwiches were offered, filled with cucumber, tomato, egg, meat or fish paste, ham, shrimps or tongue, followed by a selection of small cakes, often served on elegant silver dishes spread with lace doilies or on a three-tiered cake stand. The cakes had moved from their customary place at an elegant banquet or dinner table into the sitting room for a refined and dignified occasion. The tea was usually China or Indian, offered with milk and lemon.

Tea on the terrace on a summer afternoon. A painting by Thomas Barrell painted in the 1880s shows a silver teapot and cake stand in the fashion of the time. The repast here is still rather modest, although the British teatable was to become quite lavish within the next decade.

Towards the end of the nineteenth century and in the early decades of the twentieth century the sociable afternoon tea party developed into an elaborate repast and was finding a place on the tables of the middle and lower classes too, but as a more homely occasion, becoming a full meal rather than a social interlude. Toasted bread and tea cakes, crumpets and hot buttered scones might start the meal, followed by a selection of tasty sandwiches, and buttered tea breads, white or brown, or spiced with fruit and nuts to be spread with jam. The selection of cakes was considerable: small seed and queen cakes, pound cake, slab fruit cakes, almond-studded Dundee cake and jam-filled Victoria sponge. Small plain and almond sponges might be iced with chocolate or coffee icing and studded with a walnut or cherry. There might be maids of honour and brandy snaps filled with cream, and macaroons. All the familiar and traditional cakes of Britain would be there, and tea-time newcomers which were *petits fours* from France, genoese sponge slices filled with cream and decorated with icing and fruits, small puff pastry confections, éclairs made of choux paste and tiny, crisp, cream-filled meringues.

It also became fashionable to offer afternoon tea for particular occasions: tea on the lawn was a charming social event on a sunny afternoon, and tennis, croquet and cricket teas were popular too. Cakes were designed to represent the activity — a tennis racquet, a domino or a draughts board for instance.

Mrs Beeton recommended bridge teas, and funeral teas helped turn the thoughts of the bereaved to more frivolous matters, such as the qualities of the special bread, or the lightness of the sponge. Also in the 1920s the *thé dansant*, tea dance, appeared and became the fashion in restaurants, hotels and department stores. This was the first time young ladies might respectably attend a function outside their home without a chaperone. Tearooms were also a new venture, and the new emancipated rules applied there too.

The homely afternoon tea of the lower classes evolved into 'high tea', usually served around 6 o'clock. It marked the end of the working day in the industrial and farming communities and usually combined supper dishes with cakes and a pot of tea, so that a cooked meal later on was no longer necessary, although the day would often end with substantial bedtime snacks of pies, sandwiches, cakes and hot drinks.

'High tea' offered the same type of fare as its more elegant counterparts, but it included cold meats or pies and salads, and cold sweets such as rhubarb or apple pie, jelly or stewed fruit and trifle. Regional specialities, like lardy cake and Devonshire apple cake, might appear, while on special occasions there were iced sponges and cream-filled cakes. Many of the plainer cakes would re-appear on the following day in the working men's lunchpacks to be eaten in the mid-morning break. Biscuits and the plain cakes of old are now all that remain of this era to be served with a cup of tea or coffee.

In the 1950s, immigrant cooks from Austria and Germany had started to make their presence felt in Britain. Their pastry shops and delicatessen stores introduced a whole range of cakes, pastries and baking ingredients unfamiliar to the British pastry-cook. Gradually, as their popularity grew, their more exciting confectionery tempted the sweet tooth of the British, and gâteaux from France and torten from Austria and Hungary were offered in restaurants as dessert. In the home these lighter confections have replaced traditional puddings and desserts and are often served as a grand climax to an elegant meal.

Lardy Cake

Bread dough
475g/4¼ cups bread flour
250ml/1 cup plus 2 tbsp milk,
*   warmed to blood heat*
15g/1 tbsp fresh yeast
2 tsp salt
15g/1 tbsp lard

Filling
185g/¾ cup lard, well chilled
100g/⅓ cup light brown sugar
250g/1½ cups mixed peel
1 tsp ground mixed splice

425°F for 30-40 minutes

'Like every package of cigarettes, every lardy cake should carry a health warning', says Elizabeth David — and I couldn't agree more!

Lardy cake originates on the borders of the chalk-line in England running from Wiltshire through Oxfordshire to Cambridgeshire. It is based on a plain bread dough, enriched with a delicious sticky-sweet mixture of lard and sugar as well as dried fruits and mixed spices, and it is prepared in much the same way as puff pastry. In early times, when sugar was scarce, this was a treat reserved for harvest days and special celebrations, and, like gingerbread, was sold at local fairs. Later, when sugar dropped in price, lardy cake became very popular and could be bought from the bakery every week.

Home-made pork lard has the best flavor if you are able to obtain it.

Make a sponge batter (p. 149) with ¾ cup flour, 125ml/½ cup milk and the yeast, beat well, cover and set aside to rise and double in bulk. Sift the remaining flour and salt together into a large bowl. Rub in 15g/1 tbsp lard and make a crumb texture. Make a well in the center, pour in the risen sponge batter and most of the remaining milk. Blend well, then work and knead the dough mixture until it starts to roll off the sides of the bowl. Add a little more milk if the dough is too dry.

Turn the dough out on to a lightly floured work-surface and knead hard for about 10 minutes until it is elastic, looks shiny and throws large pockets of air. Roll it into a ball, drop it back into the mixing bowl and cover with a floured cloth. Set aside to rise in a warm place until it has doubled in bulk.

Roll the dough out on a floured work-top into a rectangle about ¼in thick. Dot about one-third of the chilled lard across the dough, to within ½in of the edges. Scatter over one-third each of the sugar and dried fruits, and a little spice. Fold one-third of the dough over from the short side into the middle (see puff pastry, p. 148), and cover with the top third of the dough. Press the sides firmly together so that the filling is completely sealed and make a quarter turn to the right; indent with two fingers. Chill in the refrigerator for 15 minutes.

Roll the dough into a rectangle as before on the indented edge, dot with half the remaining lard, sugar, fruits and spice, fold, seal and turn again; indent and chill. Repeat with the rest of the ingredients.

Finish by rolling and folding the dough to fit snugly into a deep, 8 × 10in greased baking pan. Press down well in the corners. Cover the pan with the floured cloth and leave to rise or prove and double in bulk.

Remove the cloth and brush the surface with a little milk and beaten egg, and sprinkle with granulated sugar. Score a criss-cross pattern in the surface with a sharp knife from one side to the other and bake in the pre-heated oven. Turn out of the pan to cool upside-down on a wire rack. Serve cut in slices when tepid or cold.

A Light Pound Cake

250g/1¼ cups butter
250g/1¼ cups sugar
2in vanilla pod, split
1 tsp lemon zest
4 large eggs
125g/1 cup all-purpose flour
125g/½ cup potato flour
1 tsp baking powder
1 tsp orange-flower water
1 tbsp dark rum
confectioners' sugar for
*   dredging*

350°F for 1¼ hours

Pound cake is an equal-weight cake, in which each of the main dry ingredients weighs the same as the eggs. It originated centuries ago and was highly spiced, flavored and perfumed, and filled with seeds or dried fruits. A version of pound cake may be found in almost every cookery book throughout Europe, but today's version probably tastes better than its ancestors; in the past it was necessary to beat the mixture for an hour to achieve lightness, but the refined preparation techniques and quality of the basic ingredients now make this unnecessary. Potato flour gives a finer flavor and the whipped egg white snow makes it much lighter.

Cream the butter and half the sugar until light and fluffy. Beat in the seeds of vanilla pod and the lemon zest. Beat in, one at a time, one whole egg and three of the yolks.

Sift together two or three times the flours and baking powder; then lightly beat 3 tbsp at a time into the butter and sugar mixture, taking care not to over-beat. Beat the egg whites in a separate bowl until they are firm, and beat in the rest of the sugar until the mixture looks satiny and smooth. Lighten the main mixture by beating in 2-3 spoonfuls of the meringue, then tip in the rest and gently fold in using a large metal spoon. Fold in the orange-flower water and rum.

Use a deep layer pan or gugelhupf or rehrücken mold with a 2qt capacity, or a loaf pan approximately 9 × 5 × 3in. Butter well and dust with flour. Pour in the cake mixture and smooth level. Make a slight hollow in the middle. Bake in the warmed oven until well risen and golden brown. Leave to cool in the pan for 10 minutes before turning out on to a wire rack. Dredge with confectioners' sugar before serving.

Pound cake keeps fresh for at least a week.

This basic pound cake is quite simple, but it may be enriched in a variety of exciting ways.

Try a mixture of *dried fruits* — apricots (weigh, soak in water for 2-3 hours, then dry and chop), golden raisins and raisins: 275g/2 cups altogether; you need two loaf pans for this approximately 8 × 4 × 2½in..

Mixed *candied orange, citron and lemon peel* also tastes good. *Chocolate and ginger* make the cake rich and spicy. Pour half the cake mixture into a gugelhupf mold, and to the remaining mixture add 2 tbsp cocoa powder, 1 tsp ginger powder and 50g/¼ cup preserved ginger chopped small. Blend the mixture well and spoon it on to the first quantity in the pan; gently drag a fork through it to give a marbled effect.

Probably my favorite version is one incorporating *fresh fruits*. Chose any seasonal firm fruit, but avoid soft or citrus ones: plums, grapes, apples, cherries, rhubarb, apricots and pears are all good. You will need about 750g/1½lb stone fruits, 500g/1lb others.

Wash, dry, peel and core or remove the stones. Pour half of the cake mixture into the pan and cover with a layer of fruit; spoon over the rest of the cake batter and cover with the remaining fruit. The baking time will be a little longer, and the cake will not keep for more than about 5 days.

Butter and cinnamon brown sugar crumble mixed with flaked almonds makes a delicious surprise filling. Prepare a third portion of the Streussel crumb mixture (p. 100) using light brown sugar instead of white, and mix in 50g/½ cup toasted flaked almonds. Spoon half the cake mixture into the pan and cover with the crumb filling; cover with the rest of the cake mixture and bake as usual.

LARDY CAKE (T) GINGER
SNAPS (R) YORKSHIRE
CURD TART (L): *Typical
British tea-time fare*.

Scottish Shortbread

225g/1 cup unsalted butter
110g/1 cup confectioners'
sugar, sifted
1in vanilla pod, split
2 tsp hot water
110g/1 cup all-purpose flour
110g/1/2 cup potato flour
confectioners' sugar for
dredging

325°F for 25 minutes

Makes 60 pieces

Butter shortbread originated in Scotland as a festive confection particularly for Christmas and Hogmanay. It is not unlike the plain oat-cakes eaten in Scotland all the year round. Shortbread is traditionally baked in a flat, carved wooden mold.

This method is a modern variation. Work the ingredients by hand in a chilled bowl as little and as quickly as possible. Do not use an electric mixer, which tends to over-beat and make the pastry heavy.

Cream the butter, add the confectioners' sugar and blend well. Mix in the vanilla seeds and stir in the hot water. Sift the flours together two or three times and combine lightly with the butter and sugar mixture. Gather the pastry into a ball, divide and roll into two long ropes about 3/4in in diameter. Wrap closely in plastic wrap and chill for at least 1 hour. (The pastry may be frozen at this stage for up to 2 months.) Cut 1/2in slices with a sharp knife and space 1-1 1/2in apart on a greased and floured baking sheet. Bake until slightly colored. Cool on a wire rack. Dredge with confectioners' sugar and store between sheets of wax paper in an air-tight container.

Old-fashioned Ginger Snaps

140g/1 1/4 cups all-purpose flour
1/2 tsp ground ginger
1/4 tsp allspice
120g/1/2 cup butter, chilled
140g/2/3 cup sugar
140ml/2/3 cup golden syrup
1 tbsp brandy

325°F for 6-7 minutes each
batch

Makes 30 snaps

Ginger snap dough spreads out to about five times its original size when baked. Bake only two or three at a time so that the cooked, toffee-like snap can be rolled as soon as it is lifted off the tray and before it hardens. They taste good unfilled, served with ice-cream or a creamy pudding; and for tea or coffee-time a filling of brandy-flavored whipped cream studded with candied peels is a special treat.

Sift the flour and spices two or three times together. Cut in the butter and rub to a fine crumb texture. Mix in the sugar. Add the syrup and brandy and blend into a smooth dough. The dough may be used straight away or chilled for a day so that the flavors develop.

Roll the dough into thick ropes, and pinch off walnut-sized pieces. Space two or three at a time, well apart, on a greased baking sheet and flatten a little. Bake, but watch carefully so that they do not burn. Cool for a minute or two, then lightly roll each one around the greased or oiled handle of a wooden spoon or a wooden dowel. Slide the snaps off the handle as soon as they have set and lay them on a wire rack to finish cooling.

Store between sheets of wax paper in an air-tight container for up to a week.

Simnel Cake

175g/³/₄ cup butter
175g/³/₄ light brown sugar
4 large eggs, separated
40g/¹/₃ cup ground
    almonds
1 tbsp dark rum
200g/³/₄ cups all-purpose
    flour
2 tsp mixed spice
250g/¹/₂ cups currants
165g/1 cup golden raisins
130g/³/₄ cup candied orange
    and lemon peel
confectioners' sugar for
    dredging

Marzipan layer
350g/3 cups ground almonds
350g/3 cups confectioners' sugar,
    sifted
2 tsp orange-flower water
3 drops bitter almond extract
3 egg yolks
2 tbsp apricot jam

1 egg yolk for finishing

325°F for 2 hours then 300°F
    for ¹/₂ hour

The richly fruited simnel cake that we know today originated in the late 1600s. It was baked for Mothering Sunday, which falls in mid-Lent and gave a welcome break from the Lenten fast. Mothering Sunday apparently originated in Ancient Greece as a pagan feast day of the Mother of the Gods, which in Christian times developed into worship of the Mother Church. This respect was later transferred to the mother of the family, and it became a custom in the nineteenth century for daughters working in service to travel home on Mothering Sunday bearing the gift of a simnel cake.

How marzipan came to be a part of the cake is not certain, though 'marchpane' was considered a great delicacy in the seventeenth century and was used mostly for religious and festive baking. The traditional marzipan balls decorating the top of the cake are said to represent the twelve apostles.

Since the beginning of this century, simnel cake has been regarded as an Easter cake, and Mothering Sunday, though not forgotten, has fallen prey to commercial exploitation and its religious significance has been lost.

This recipe is based on the most recent version of simnel cake.

Make the marzipan first. Combine the almonds and confectioners' sugar in a bowl, add the flower water, almond extract and egg yolks, and knead to a smooth firm paste. Roll into a ball, wrap and chill.

Prepare a 3in deep layer cake pan (8in in diameter), butter and line with wax paper and butter the paper.

Beat the butter and sugar until light and fluffy, beat in the egg yolks one at a time, add the almonds and rum. Sift the flour and spices together, then lightly mix about one-third of it into the egg batter. Combine the dried fruits and candied peels. Beat the egg whites in a clean bowl, until they stand in firm peaks and lightly fold them into the main mixture, alternating with siftings of flour and portions of dried fruits and peels. Pour half the mixture into the prepared baking pan.

On a board dusted with sifted confectioners' sugar roll one-third of the marzipan into a circle 7in in diameter. Lay it on top of the cake mixture in the tin and press down lightly. Pour on the remainder of the batter, smooth level and make a small hollow in the center.

Set the cake pan on a baking tray and bake in the preheated oven. Reduce the heat after 2 hours and cover the cake with two sheets of wax paper to prevent the top from browning too much. Bake until it starts to shrink away slightly from the sides of the pan. Test with a skewer for readiness. Leave in the pan to settle for 15 minutes then turn out on to a wire rack to cool.

To finish the cake heat 2 tbsp apricot jam with the same amount of water until thickened. Strain and cool. Brush the apricot on the top of the cake only.

Roll out the remaining marzipan to fit the top of the cake, and trim neatly. Make 12 small balls with the left-over scraps. Lightly press the squared mesh of a wire rack into the marzipan layer; fix the marzipan balls on the edge of the cake with a dab of beaten egg yolk. Brush the whole of the surface with egg yolk.

Push the cake under a hot broiler and toast the marzipan for 3-4 minutes to a golden color but watching all the time so that it does not burn.

The cake keeps fresh in an air-tight container for 2 months. Dredge a little confectioners' sugar over just before serving. Serve it on Easter day with a glass of sweet white wine or a Riesling wine; or on Mothering Sunday.

SIMNEL CAKE: *It is now customary to serve this cake at Eastertime, but in the past it was traditionally baked as a gift for mothers on Mother's Day.*

Spiced Apple Tart

1 portion sweet shortcrust
   pastry (p. 145) for an 8in tart
   pan

Filling
500g/1lb cooking or Golden
   Delicious apples
2in cinnamon stick
15g/1 tbsp butter
$^1/_2$ tsp ground nutmeg
75g/$^1/_3$ cup sugar
1 tbsp sugar and $^1/_2$ tsp ground
   cinnamon for dredging
whipped cream or custard to
   serve

400°F for 10 minutes then
   reduce the temperature to
   350°F for approximately 40
   minutes

Peel, core and slice the apples thickly. Place them in a pan with the cinnamon stick, butter and 6 tbsp water. Bring to a simmer then stew until tender. Draw off the heat, stir in the nutmeg and sugar and leave to cool. Remove the cinnamon stick. Meanwhile make the pastry (p. 145). Divide it into one-third and two-thirds and roll out the smaller piece to fit the tart pan, leaving it to rest for a few minutes. Lift up the pastry using the rolling pin as an aid, and line the pan with it. Trim the edge and prick all over with a fork.

Spoon the cold apple mixture into the shell, mounding it high in the middle and leaving a wide border of pastry all round the rim of the dish. Moisten the pastry rim with water. Roll out the remainder of the pastry and lay it on top of the apple filling. Pinch and crimp the two pastry edges well together,

trim the sides and decorate with left over scraps of pastry. Make two small cuts in the middle of the crust to allow the steam to escape. Place the tart pan on a hot baking sheet in the preheated oven and bake the tart for 10 minutes, then reduce the temperature and bake until golden. Dredge the top generously with a mixture of 1 tbsp sugar and $^1/_2$ tsp ground cinnamon. Set the plate to cool on a wire rack.

Serve hot or cold with whipped cream or custard on the side.

Other fillings are made with rhubarb, gooseberries, blueberries, blackberries — they also taste splendid mixed with apples — and blackcurrants. These fruits do not need pre-cooking.

Lemon Meringue Pie

8$^1/_2$in sweet shortcrust pastry
   case, baked blind (p. 145)
sugar for dredging

Lemon curd
zest and juice of 3 lemons
165g/$^2/_3$ cup plus 1 tbsp sugar
75g/$^1/_3$ cup unsalted butter,
   softened and cubed
2 large eggs

Meringue
2 egg whites
110g/$^1/_2$ cup sugar

350°F for 10 minutes, then
   reduce the oven temperature
   to 300°F for 45 minutes

Using a wooden spoon, crush the lemon zest and sugar in a heat-proof bowl. Strain in the lemon juice and add the butter cubes. Set the bowl over a pan of simmering water and leave the butter to melt and the sugar to dissolve. Meanwhile beat the 2 eggs in a separate bowl until frothy and strain them into the lemon mixture. Blend all the ingredients carefully and cook slowly, stirring often, until the mixture thickens to a creamy consistency. Draw off the heat, lightly rub a little butter over the surface to prevent a skin forming and set aside to cool.

Pour the lemon curd into the cooled pastry shell and level out. Place the pie in the heated oven to warm and set the filling.

Make the meringue (p. 140). Lift the flan

out of the oven and reduce the temperature of the oven. Quickly spoon the meringue on to the lemon filling and dredge with sugar. Replace the pie in the oven and bake until the meringue peaks are crisp and have turned a golden brown color.

Serve warm or cold.

Yorkshire Curd Tart

1 portion sweet shortcrust
pastry (p. 145) for a 8¹/₂in
loose-bottomed tart pan
110g/¹/₂ cup butter
50g/¹/₄ cup sugar
1 tsp lemon zest
250g/1 cup curds cheese, sieved
2 eggs, separated
110g/³/₄ cup raisins
pinch salt
¹/₂ tsp ground nutmeg
1 tbsp ground almonds or
toasted breadcrumbs

400°F for 15 minutes then
325°F for 15 minutes

An early English recipe.

Butter the pan and line with the pastry; prick all over with a fork. Chill. Cream the butter and sugar until light and fluffy, mix in the lemon zest, curds cheese, egg yolks and raisins. Add the salt and nutmeg. Beat the egg whites separately until they are firm and lightly fold them into the mixture. Scatter the almonds or breadcrumbs over the pastry base. Pour the cheese filling into the pastry case, and bake until golden and the pastry is brown. Leave to cool on a wire rack in the pan.

The tart will freeze well for up to 2 months.

POUND CAKE: *This version of a centuries-old recipe is layered with a filling of butter, cinnamon and brown sugar crumble.*

RHUBARB TART (*apple tart*): *this is a variation of the spiced apple tart recipe on page 48. Rhubarb pieces may be dredged with sugar and left overnight to draw the juices. Flavor with 2 teaspoonfuls of orange zest. Drain the excess juices before continuing as in the recipe for spiced apple tart.*

Cornish Saffron Bread

½ tsp whole saffron filaments
150ml/⅔ cup water, warmed
    to blood heat
300g/2 cups currants
100g/¾ cup golden raisins
65g/⅓ cup chopped candied
    orange and lemon peel
150g/1¼ cups all-purpose
    flour, sifted
50g/¼ cup sugar
150ml/⅔ cup milk, warmed to
    blood heat
20g/1oz (scant) fresh yeast
375g/3¼ cups bread flour
1 tsp salt
pinch ground nutmeg
pinch ground cinnamon
pinch mixed spice
75g/⅓ cup butter
75g/⅓ cup lard
2 tbsp milk plus 1 tbsp sugar
    for brushing

425°F for 30 minutes

Makes two 9 × 5 × 3in
    (2qt) loaves

Saffron is the bright fiery-red stamen of the *Crocus sativus*. It has always been the most expensive spice in the world, and it was especially favored in Middle Eastern dishes for both its pungent and exotic flavor and its color. Introduced to England during the sixteenth century, it grew in North Cornwall and Saffron Waldon, Essex, until quite recently. The spicy cake is a yeasted, lightly fruited dough usually made without eggs.

Always buy whole saffron stamens rather than powder, which may be adulterated.

Dry the saffron filaments in a hot oven for 5 minutes, then crumble them into a cup filled with the hot water and leave to infuse while you prepare the other ingredients.

Place the dried fruits and peel in a large bowl and set it in the warm, switched-off oven to heat through.

Make a yeast sponge batter (p. 149) with the all-purpose flour, 2 tsp sugar, the milk and yeast; beat well, cover and leave to rise and double in bulk.

Sift the flour with the salt and spices into a large bowl. Cut in the butter and lard and rub to a crumb texture. Mix in the rest of the sugar. Make a well in the center and pour in the yeast batter and saffron liquid. Draw in the flour mixture and beat into a soft dough. Mix in the warmed fruits and peel. Blend thoroughly until the dough is shiny and shows large air bubbles. Cover the bowl with a floured cloth, stand it in a warm place and leave to rise until it doubles in bulk, which may take as long as 2 hours.

Knock back the dough and knead for a moment or two, then divide it equally between two lightly greased 9 × 5 × 3in loaf pans. Pat into shape and leave to rise for up to 1 hour more until risen to almost the top of the tin. Bake immediately in the hot oven.

As soon as they are removed from the oven brush the loaves with a warmed mixture of 2 tbsp milk and 1 tbsp sugar. Leave in the pans for 15 minutes before turning out to cool on a wire rack.

Serve saffron bread as soon as it has cooled. You may like to freeze one loaf while it is still warm.

Flapjacks

110g/½ cup butter
75g/⅓ cup light brown sugar
75ml/⅓ cup golden syrup
¾ tsp ground ginger
175g/2 cups rolled oats
50g/½ cup flaked almonds

350°F for 15-20 minutes

Heat gently the butter, sugar and syrup in a small pan until the butter has melted and the sugar dissolved. Stir until smooth. Draw off the heat and stir in the ginger, oats and almonds. Spread the mixture out in a buttered 13½ × 9½in jelly roll pan. Bake until golden, taking care that it does not scorch; it should still feel quite soft to the touch. Cut into fingers in the pan with a buttered knife while still hot. They harden and crisp as they cool. Leave to cool in the tin. Flapjacks keep well in an air-tight container.

'Plumb Cake'

A RICH FRUIT CAKE FOR CHRISTMAS

300g/2 cups currants
300g/2 cups raisins
140g/³/₄ cup orange and lemon
     candied peels, chopped
4 tbsp sherry or madeira
4 tbsp brandy
350g/3³/₄ cups unsalted buttter
     plus extra for greasing
225g/1 cup brown sugar, light
     or dark
5 large egg yolks
140g/1¹/₄ cups ground almonds
1 tsp orange-flower water
285g/2¹/₂ cups all-purpose flour
¹/₂ tsp ground cloves
1 tsp ground nutmeg
1 tsp ground cinnamon
pinch ground ginger
3 large egg whites

300°F for 1¹/₂ hours then lower
     the temperature to 275°F
     for 3-3¹/₂ hours

Mix the dried fruits and peels with the sherry or madeira and brandy. Leave to soak for 1 hour while you prepare the other ingredients.

Line the base and sides of a deep, loose-based 8-8¹/₂in deep layer cake pan with two layers of brown or wax paper, and finish with a third sheet of wax standing with a 2in high collar above the side of the pan. Grease well with butter.

Beat the unsalted butter and sugar until light and fluffy. Beat in the egg yolks one at a time, mixing well between each addition. Beat in the ground almonds and orange-flower water. Sift the flour with the ground spices and baking powder and set aside. Beat the egg whites in a clean bowl until they stand in firm, snowy peaks, then fold about one-third into the main mixture with alternate siftings of the flour and spices. Continue until all is incorporated, but avoid over-beating. Mix in the dried fruits and liquids until well blended.

Pour the mixture into the prepared cake pan; smooth the surface and make a hollow in the middle so that it will bake flat. Place the pan on a flat baking sheet that has been lined with two sheets of brown paper to give added protection, and bake in the preheated oven as instructed. If the top appears to be browning too much, cover it with a sheet of brown paper. Test the cake for readiness.

Leave the cake to cool in the pan, set on a wire rack. Strip off the papers the following day and wrap in clean paper before storing in an air-tight tin.

For a strong spirituous flavor, the cake may be unwrapped and fed with 2 tbsp of brandy each week.

MARZIPAN

5 tbsp apricot jam
250g/2 cups pecan or
     walnut halves
140g/5oz glacé cherries
50g/2oz crystallized angelica or
     other candied fruits of your
     choice

It is traditional to cover a Christmas cake with a layer of marzipan and decorate it with a coating of white royal icing. The following decoration is more unusual — you may lay it on a base of marzipan too if you like.

Heat the apricot jam with 3 tbsp water and cook until thickened. Strain.

Place the cake on a wire rack. Brush apricot jam all over the top of the cake. Embed the prepared fruits and nuts in a random pattern. Finish by brushing more apricot jam over all the fruits and nuts, to give a high sheen. When the apricot coating has set, tie a wide ribbon or paper frill around the cake and place it on an elegant plate or silver board to serve.

The cake should be stored in an air-tight container and will keep fresh for several weeks.

PLUMB CAKE: *A traditional Christmas cake with an unusual decoration of glacé fruits and pecan nuts.*

SAFFRON BREAD: *Saffron used to be the most expensive spice in the world, and often turmeric was sold in its stead; but there is no mistaking saffron's very dominant and distinctive taste.*

FLAPJACKS: *A baking hint: as soon as the sugar stops bubbling on the surface, the flapjacks are ready to come out of the oven.*

AUSTRIA & HUNGARY

The foundation of the House of Habsburg in 1292 saw the beginning of a powerful dynasty, which, after a number of cleverly planned marriages and some warmongering, greatly enlarged its territories. The Empire extended from as far as central Russia and the Black Sea, to the Adriatic Sea and at various times it encompassed Spain, Italy, Switzerland parts of southern Germany and France, and the Netherlands. But it was towards the end of its existence, in the seventeenth and eighteenth centuries, the Baroque era, that the Empire achieved its zenith in grand living.

Apart from their geographical proximity, it is fascinating that two such dissimilar nations as the Austrians and the Hungarians should be so closely bound together. The early Hungarians who settled in the valley of the Danube were 'spiritually and materially Asiatics', who had migrated southwards, partly through Turkey. Of nomadic peasant stock, they were courageous, with a tribal spirit of kinsmanship and a spontaneous *joie de vivre*. Their gipsy traditions, steeped in the mysticism of the Orient and bound by folklore, gave them an uncomplicated outlook on life. The Austrians, and principally the Viennese, on the other hand, were greatly influenced by the sophisticated, elegant lifestyle and culture of the great cities of the West, especially of France. But the geographical position of Vienna was also a vital factor in its development. The city stands at a natural crossroads in a valley between the mountains, and during the first millennium, suffered the depravations of various marauding tribes as they swept across Europe. Despite these traumas, the Viennese profited from their unwelcome visitors and absorbed an exciting *mélange* of traditions, arts and crafts, music and cuisine. Later Vienna established itself as an important trading centre and benefited from many new and exciting foodstuffs, particularly spices and sugarcane, which the Crusaders brought from the East on their homeward journeys. Late in the century (1697), the Habsburgs conquered Hungary and the surrounding states of Romania, Czechoslavakia and Yugoslavia, and Vienna became the powerful and wealthy capital. This was the start of an uneasy political alliance, but it was also the start of a gastronomic alliance with an outstanding pastry cuisine that still remains today as undisputed head of the 'pastry kingdom'.

Somehow the flamboyant and sumptuous style of the Baroque era, usually associated only with architecture, music, painting and sculpture, affected the whole mode of living. Life became an indulgent extravaganza. Eating, drinking and merrymaking were of prime importance to rich and poor alike, and although the basic food of the wealthy and the aristocracy was considerably influenced by the local peasant and pastoral traditions, it was greatly embellished and enriched by the choice of luxurious ingredients. Vienna was also eager to absorb the best that other European cultures had to offer.

A typical banquet of the time consisted of eight courses, and several of the dishes would reflect different ethnic origins; but the predilection for sugary confections was particularly evident. This love of sweet foods already existed in the early 1500s when guilds of various 'sweet' craftsmen were founded. Each craftsman was allowed to prepare only the speciality for which he was trained. Sugar bakers worked with burnt sugar and almonds, biscuits and *Zwieback* (a type of rusk); the *Lebzelter* made only honey and spiced *Lebkuchen*. Chocolate makers handled only chocolate, and there were marzipan manufacturers, cake bakers, sweet makers and different classes of bread-bakers too.

In the seventeenth and eighteenth centuries the luxurious cakes and pastries graced only the tables of the aristocracy; but by the nineteenth century, as the price of sugar dropped with the introduction of sugar beet and as spices became more readily available, everyone was able to afford them.

By this time (much to the chagrin of the pastry chefs), coffee-houses had become popular, although coffee had been enjoyed in Austria since 1683 when the Turks had beseiged Vienna — Vienna had won the battle and their coffee too. Instead of the pastry-shops, coffee-houses became the meeting-place, principally for men, who came to exchange news and gossip, to read the daily papers or to play chess, billiards or cards, and, most important of all, to drink the favorite *mélange mit Schlag*, coffee with milk and whipped cream, with a glass of water. (Cream was a great Viennese favorite and had been discovered, it is said, about 200 years earlier.) A small selection of cakes and pastries was also offered.

The life of the ordinary people on the land naturally differed from that of the wealthy townsfolk. They worked and played hard, but ate well, usually taking five meals a day, which were established by the daily schedule of the farming communities. Three main meals and a mid-morning and afternoon break, the *Jause*, which generally consisted of bread, cheese and cold meats, or leftovers from a previous meal, and was often followed by a *Mehlspeise*. This warm, sweet dish (in early times it did not include sugar) was composed principally of flour (*Mehl*), eggs, butter and milk, and often included nuts or fruits. It is still a favourite in these regions today. In early times, before sugar was available, every meal would be followed by a *Mehlspeise*, and the elegant households employed a cook who specialized in their preparation. The cook was always a woman — men specialized in cakes and pastries — all the wonderful noodles, dumplings, baked puddings and pancakes came from these kitchens. Best known in the *Mehlspeisköchins* repertoire was the *strudel*, with its Middle Eastern origins, but which we all now associate with Austria and Hungary.

As the Habsburg powers decayed towards the end of the nineteenth century, a more casual and relaxed lifestyle became fashionable. While the preoccupation with good eating and drinking persisted, the preparation of food became simpler, and it was less rich. But *Mehlspeisen*, cakes and pastries remained as popular as ever.

The Viennese *Kaffeejause* or *Kaffeeklatsch*, unlike its simple country counterparts, now became a very sophisticated affair. Between 5 and 7 p.m. in the afternoon fashionable hostesses would set their tables with the most elegant *Jausegedeck* of table linen and best porcelain. Savory snacks, sandwiches and canapés were offered, first with a glass of wine and then cakes and pastries were served with coffee. Usually the cakes were a *Gugelhupf* or *Bischofsbrod* and the pastries included doughnuts, walnut and poppy seed crescents, horns and *Streusselkuchen*. There were small, yeasted pastries, filled with nuts and curds cheese, or plainer shortcrust pastries and cookies. *Linzertorte* and *Sachertorte* were the most popular large cakes, but cream-filled cakes or heavily fruited tarts were rarely offered.

The less affluent baked at home for Christmas and other festivals — the ritual of preparation embraced the whole family and began weeks ahead of time. There were all the Christmas specialities: stars and crescents, horns and hearts and the little spiced cookies, perfuming the air with honey, exotic spices, lemons, almonds and fresh vanilla pod. It was a time for hospitality that extended to every friend and relative at any time of the day, and the baked delicacies would be taken as gifts.

DER GRABEN. *This is one of the oldest streets in Vienna now flanked by the most luxurious and expensive shops and cafés. The Graben was originally a walled moat, but disappeared when the city was enlarged in 1220. In the eighteenth century, during the reign of Maria Therese, the Graben became the focal point of all sophisticated and elegant Viennese life.*

There are hundreds of coffee houses and candy shops in Vienna; among the best known are Aïda, Gerstner, Heiner, Janele and Lehmann. Christoph Demel's Söhne in the Kohlmarkt has the finest reputation among pastry shops in the world. It was founded in 1786 by Ludwig Dehne, whose widow was later chosen as court caterer and official sugar baker of the imperial household. In 1857 Christoph Demel took over the shop and moved the premises to the Kohlmarkt.

The end of the nineteenth century and the start of this century saw in Vienna a continuation of the over-indulgent and extravagant lifestyle. The elegant Hotel Sacher was a meeting place for royalty, the rich and the famous; and Demel's pastry shop too, was a favorite rendezvous. The period saw the publication of many new cookery books, which included substantial sections on *Mehlspeisen* and pastry cookery. These books were intended not for the court baker, as in the past, but for the housewife, for, since the dramatic fall in sugar prices, the exciting cakes that had hitherto been exclusive to the wealthy and in the pastry shops, could now be baked at home. With zeal, the housewives siezed the opportunity and continued the sweet gastronomic tradition in true Austro-Hungarian style. The riches of the court now graced the tables of the humble.

Baking in Austria and Hungary still reflects the ethnic influences of its visitors from the past, but these have now been almost entirely absorbed and become the nations' own. Nut cakes are notable, and in fact, nuts often replace flour in recipes that rely on egg yolks and beaten whites to give lightness to the mixture. Dried fruit cakes contain pears, plums, figs and dates, as well as the more familiar fruits. Artificial raising agents are not used, but the natural leaven of yeast is much in evidence.

Vienna always had a fondness for whipped cream, and by the nineteenth century it started to appear in layered cakes and with the invention of more sophisticated piping equipment, decoration became more elaborate.

Both countries still love strudel, which is enriched with fillings of fruits, cheeses and nuts, but in Hungary sour cream takes the place of the Austrian whipped cream. It may accompany any meal and is an unusual addition to a fine pastry or filling.

In Austro-Hungarian baking, whether the cake is plain and simple, or filled with walnuts or poppy seed or cream, plums, cherries, honey or liqueur, the taste is enhanced by complementary flavors; and the decoration, whether grand or simple, is an extension of the goodness inside, the essence of Austrian and Hungarian pastries.

59

AUSTRIA

*Gugelhupf Dattel Torte Dunkle Mandeltorte Bischofbrod
Walnut Torte Sachertorte Germ Kipfel Linzertorte
Habsburger Torte Floretiner Kaffeetorte Topfen Kuchen
Punschtorte Orangen Torte Nonnen Bretzerln
Vanille Kipferln*

Gugelhupf

50ml/¹/₄ cup milk, warmed to blood heat
10g/¹/₂oz fresh yeast
140g/1 cup plus 1¹/₂ tbsp bread flour
50g/¹/₄ cup sugar
75g/¹/₃ cup butter
1 tsp grated lemon zest
6 egg yolks
100g/¹/₄ cup raisins
2 tbsp kirsch
1 tsp corn oil
2 egg whites
confectioners' sugar for dredging
25g/¹/₄ cup pine nuts (optional)

375°F for 30 minutes

It is difficult to attribute Gugelhupf to any one country as it has remained popular throughout the Teutonic lands for centuries. It is probably related to the Russian *kulich* and the Slavonic *baba*, but the name comes from the mold in which the cake is baked: an unusual utensil, with sloping and molded, patterned sides and a central funnel. Simple, early models were made of tin, but more elaborate embossed ones of fired clay or copper were used for special occasions. Today they are usually made of aluminum or copper and are available in many specialist kitchen shops.

The most common version of the cake itself is made with yeast. It is sometimes rather bland and plain, like a bread, and is served for breakfast, but other versions are much richer and are filled with dried fruits, nuts and eggs. Each region has its own variation.

The following recipe is very rich and was baked for the Austro-Hungarian Imperial court. It is made with many egg yolks, and, unusually, the mixture is prepared like a sponge. Gugelhupf is very light and fluffy and is a pleasant accompaniment to coffee or tea or even a glass of sweet wine.

Carefully brush with melted butter a 9in gugelhupf mold and dust with flour; drop the pine nuts, if used, in the bottom.

Make a sponge batter (p. 149) with the warm milk, yeast, 2 tbsp flour and 1 tsp sugar taken from the main mixture; beat well. Cover and set aside for about 10 minutes to rise and double in bulk.

Cream the butter with the sugar and lemon zest until thick and fluffy. Beat in the egg yolks one at a time, beating thoroughly between each addition. Mix in the sponge batter and a quarter of the remaining flour and continue beating for about 10 minutes by machine (20 minutes by hand). The mixture should be well aerated and have thickened.

Dust the raisins with a little flour and blend them into the mixture. Stir in the kirsch and the oil. Beat the egg whites in a separate, clean bowl until they hold firm, glossy peaks. Lightly fold them into the main mixture, with alternate siftings of flour, until all is well combined. Pour the yeast dough into the prepared mold and set it in a warm place to rise and at least double in bulk; it should rise to almost the top of the pan and this takes about 1¹/₂ hours.

Bake in the preheated oven until well browned and turn out onto a wire rack to cool. Dredge with confectioners' sugar to serve. Freeze while still warm. Defrost at room temperature for 3-4 hours.

Dattel Torte

Pastry
100g/³/₄ cup plus 1 tbsp all-
  purpose flour
50g/¹/₄ cup butter
50g/¹/₄ cup sugar
2 egg yolks

Filling
240g/8oz fresh dates with
  stones (7oz pitted)
80g/¹/₃ cup chopped candied
  orange and lemon peel
240g/1¹/₂ cups unblanched,
  finely chopped almonds
4 egg whites
240g/1 cup sugar

400°F for 15 minutes then
  reduce the oven temperature
  to 350°F for 1 hour

Sift the flour into a bowl. Make a well in the middle and cut in the butter. Lightly rub to a fine crumb texture and mix in the sugar. Add the egg yolks and blend to a smooth pastry. Roll into a ball, wrap in plastic wrap and chill for 30 minutes. Roll out the pastry and line the base of a greased 9¹/₂in spring-form pan. Weigh down with pastry pebbles and par-bake for 15 minutes (p. 145) until set but barely colored. Leave to cool on a wire rack. Lower the oven temperature.

Skin the dates and remove the stones. Roll the dates in a little flour to prevent them from sticking to the fingers and cut them into thin strips. Mix them with the chopped peel and chopped almonds. Beat the egg whites until they stand in firm snowy peaks, sift in the sugar and beat for 2-3 minutes until the mixture is very firm with glossy peaks.

Lightly fold the chopped fruits into the meringue mixture and pour into the par-baked pastry shell. Bake in the preheated oven.

To serve cover the top of the cake with whipped cream and decorate with flaked, toasted almonds and date slivers; or glaze with a lemon or punch-flavored icing (p. 157).

Dunkle Mandeltorte

DARK ALMOND CAKE

65g/5 tbsp butter
4 hard-boiled egg yolks
250g/1²/₃ cups unblanched
  almonds, ground slightly
  coarse
250g/1 cup plus 2 tbsp sugar
1 tsp lemon zest
1 tbsp lemon juice
1 whole egg
1 egg yolk
¹/₂ tsp cinnamon powder
25g/3 tbsp all-purpose flour

350°F for 1 hour

The unusual proportions in the blend of ingredients give this cake a rather crunchy, chewy texture, and the flavor of the raw almonds, combined with lemon and cinnamon, makes it quite special. The secret of its success lies in the long but essential period of beating during preparation.

Cream the butter and mix in the hard-boiled egg yolks; beat well. Add the remaining ingredients and beat the mixture very thoroughly for about 15 minutes by machine (30 minutes by hand). Pour into a greased and floured 8¹/₂in spring-form pan and bake in the preheated oven until risen and well browned. Place the pan on a wire rack and unmold after 10 minutes to finish cooling. The cake will keep fresh for several weeks. Serve it in small slices as it is very rich and delicious.

DATTELTORTE: *Fresh dates may be bought only in the winter months. Otherwise use dried, pitted dates, but cook them first in a little water for a short while to soften them.*

Walnut Torte

4 eggs, separated
110g/$\frac{1}{2}$ cup sugar
225g/2 cups ground walnuts
50g/$\frac{1}{2}$ cup unblanched, ground almonds
1 tbsp toasted bread crumbs plus extra for the pan
1 tbsp cocoa powder
1 tsp instant coffee
confectioners' sugar for dredging

350°F for 50 minutes

Beat the egg yolks and sugar until pale, creamy and well expanded. Mix the walnuts with the almonds, bread crumbs and cocoa and instant coffee and blend well with the egg yolk mixture. Beat the egg whites until they are firm and beat 4 tbsp into the main mixture to lighten it. Carefully fold in the rest of the egg snow. Pour the batter into a buttered and breadcrumbed 8$\frac{1}{2}$in spring-form pan and bake immediately. Leave to cool in the pan for 10 minutes before turning out on to a wire rack.

Dredge with confectioners' sugar to serve. For a more elaborate occasion, brush with warm strained apricot jam and cover with a coffee or chocolate flavored fondant or glacé icing (p. 154 or p. 157). Decorate with a few walnut halves while the icing is still warm.

WALNUT TORTE: *A simple nut cake with a good strong flavor; it keeps well for up to two weeks.*

Bischofbrod

BISHOP'S BREAD

70g/¹/₃ cup butter
70g/¹/₃ cup sugar
5 egg yolks
75g/³/₄ cup all-purpose flour,
    sifted
1 tsp orange zest
25g/2 tbsp pine nuts
25g/2 tbsp raisins
25g/2 tbsp golden raisins
25g/1oz dark bittersweet
    chocolate, cut in small pieces
4 egg whites

350°F for 1 hour

A simple bread to serve with tea or coffee.

Beat the butter and sugar until pale and fluffy. Beat in the egg yolks one at a time, adding 1 tsp of the flour if necessary to prevent the mixture from curdling. Mix in the orange zest and pine nuts. Dust the raisins and golden raisins with a little flour, taken from the main quantity, and combine them with the mixture. Mix in the chocolate pieces. Beat up the egg whites until they stand in firm snowy peaks and lightly fold them into the mixture. Lastly sift in the flour in three stages and combine gently.

Pour the mixture into a buttered rehrücken mold or a 9 × 5 × 3in (2qt) loaf pan lined with wax paper. Bake until well risen and golden. Turn out of the pan to cool on a wire rack. Keep for 2 days before cutting. The loaf will stay fresh for about 10 days.

Florentiner Kaffeetorte

COFFEE SPONGE

5 tsp instant coffee
4 eggs, separated
65g/5 tbsp sugar
2in vanilla pod, split
50g/¹/₂ cup ground almonds
2 tbsp all-purpose flour, sifted
butter, flour and sugar for the
    pan
140ml/²/₃ cup heavy or
    whipping cream
2 tbsp light cream (optional)
2 tbsp sugar
2-3 tbsp coffee liqueur or dark
    rum
chocolate coffee beans and
    grated chocolate to decorate

350°F for 30 minutes

An airy, light coffee sponge with a rich alcoholic tang.

Dissolve the instant coffee in 1¹/₂ tsp boiling water and leave to cool. Beat the egg yolks and sugar until thick, pale and creamy. Beat in the seeds of vanilla, ground almonds and about two-thirds of the coffee liquid. Beat the egg whites until they stand in firm, snowy peaks and fold them into the main mixture in two stages, alternating with siftings of flour. Pour the batter into a buttered, flour- and sugar-dusted 8¹/₂in spring-form pan and bake until well risen and brown. Leave to settle in the tin for 10 minutes before turning out to cool on a wire rack.

Beat the cream to hold soft peaks and beat in the sugar, remaining coffee liquid and liqueur.
Split the cooled cake in half and spread half the cream on the base. Cover with the top layer and smooth over the rest of the cream. Decorate with chocolate coffee beans and grated chocolate. Chill before serving.

Nonnen Bretzerln

NUN'S PRETZELS

2 tbsp butter
1 small egg
50g/¹/₄ cup confectioners' sugar
100ml/7 tsbp heavy cream
175g/1¹/₂ cup all-purpose flour,
*   sifted*
egg white for brushing
coarse sugar for sprinkling

400°F for 20 minutes

Makes 25-30 pieces

Beat the butter and egg until creamy. Mix in the sugar and cream. Sieve most of the flour on to the work-top, make a well in the center and drop in the mixture. Combine the ingredients to make a smooth pastry. Roll into a ball, wrap in plastic wrap and chill for at least 30 minutes. Divide the dough into two and leave half in the refrigerator while you work with the other.

Pinch off walnut-sized pieces of dough, and lightly roll each into a rope about ¹/₄in thick and 9in long, slightly tapered at the ends. To shape the pretzel, lift up both ends and cross them over in the center by pressing both the ends lightly on the top of the roll. Place on a greased and floured baking sheet. Finish the rest of the dough in the same way.

Brush the pastries with lightly beaten egg white and sprinkle with a little coarse sugar. Bake in the preheated oven until only just colored. Cool on a wire rack. Serve with coffee. Stored in an air-tight container, pretzels will keep fresh for several weeks.

Germ Kipfel

YEASTED CRESCENTS

15g/¹/₂oz fresh yeast
50ml/¹/₄ cup milk, warmed to
*   blood heat*
20g/1¹/₂ tbsp sugar
130g/1 cup plus 1¹/₂ tbsp bread
*   flour, sifted*
pinch salt
2 small egg yolks
70g/¹/₃ cup butter

Walnut filling
50g/¹/₄ cup sugar
1 tbsp milk
130g/1 cup ground walnuts
1 tsp lemon zest
1 small dessert apple, peeled
*   and grated*

375°F for 20 minutes

Makes 15 crescents

Kipfel are a traditional favorite pastry in Austria. A charming legend attached to them suggests that they were first baked in Vienna, in 1683, during the Turkish seige of the city. The crescent, in imitation of their invaders' emblem, was the Austrian gesture of defiance. (In fact the crescent symbol had religious origins some centuries earlier.)

Prepare the yeast sponge (p. 149) with the yeast, warm milk, 1 tsp sugar and 2 tbsp flour taken from the main quantity; blend and beat well. Cover and set aside to rise.

Sift the rest of the flour with the salt into a large warm bowl and make a well in the center. Drop in the lightly beaten egg yolks, the butter cut in pieces and the sugar. Draw a little flour in from the sides and pour in the sponge batter. Combine all the ingredients by beating at first, then kneading, until the dough is very elastic and large bubbles of air start to form. Cover with a cloth and leave in a warm place for 1-2 hours to rise and double in volume.

Knock the dough back and roll it out on a floured board to ¹/₈in thick. Cut into 4in triangles and place a spoonful of filling (see below) in the center of each. Roll the pastry up starting from the base line, bending it into a crescent shape. Lay the pastries on a greased and floured baking sheet and brush them with lightly beaten egg.

Cover the pastries with a lightly floured cloth and leave to rise for a further 30-40 minutes until they have doubled in size. Brush again with beaten egg and bake in the warmed oven until risen and golden. Cool on a wire rack and dredge with confectioners' sugar to serve.

Prepare the filling following the instructions on p. 76 for Poppy Seed or Walnut Roll.

HABSBURGER TORTE: A typical, elaborately decorated Austro-Hungarian confection made of hazelnut and chocolate sponges that are filled with chocolate cream and pistachio and almond cream.

FLORENTINER
KAFFEETORTE: *This is one
of those cakes that
disappears almost as quickly
as it is cut.*

SACHERTORTE: *This is
usually undecorated, but
here chocolate leaves and
flakes add interest. To make
chocolate leaves, gently melt
the chocolate, then drag
clean, freshly picked leaves
through it. Peel off the leaf
when the chocolate has
cooled and set.*

Linzertorte

JAM TART

165g/1¼ cups all-purpose
    flour, sifted
200g/¾ cup plus 1 tbsp butter
200g/¾ cup plus 1 tbsp sugar
200g/1⅓ cups unblanched
    almonds, or toasted
    hazelnuts, ground slightly
    coarse
1 tsp ground cinnamon
2 tsp lemon zest
3 egg yolks
1 tbsp lemon juice
250g/¾ cup raspberry or
    redcurrant jam
egg yolk for brushing
confectioners' sugar for
    dredging

400°F for 30-40 minutes

Until the Sachertorte ousted it from popularity, Linzertorte was always the favorite cake for festivals and celebrations during the eighteenth and nineteenth centuries. Almonds, the main ingredient, were coveted from early times and brought as valuable trading cargo from the east along with spices.

It was not until the beginning of the eighteenth century that Linzertorte was actually named. The pastry is traditionally made with ground almonds, filled with a preserve and decorated with a trellis pattern.

Sift the flour on to the work-top and make a well in the middle. Cut in the butter and blend together to a fine crumb texture. Mix in the sugar, ground nuts, cinnamon and lemon zest. Combine to a smooth pastry with the egg yolks and lemon juice. Blend the dough, roll into a ball, wrap in plastic film and chill for 1 hour.

Roll out half the pastry on a floured board and line the base and ½in up the sides of an ungreased 9½in spring-form pan or tart pan. Prick the base all over with a fork and spread a thick, even layer of jam over the base. Roll out the rest of the pastry ⅛in thick, and use a fluted pastry wheel to cut long narrow strips about ½in wide. Start making the trellis by laying the pastry strips across the jam surface. Lay one piece straight down the middle and evenly space four more strips on either side. Lay further strips in the same way across at right angles. Reserve some for the edges.

Brush all the pastry strips with beaten egg and, to give a neat finish, lay a long strip of pastry all around the side of the pan over the edges of the trellis. The egg helps seal the joints. Brush the edge with egg.

Bake the Linzertorte in the preheated oven. Dot a little more jam into each lattice hole and leave to cool in the tin on a wire rack. Dredge with confectioners' sugar and serve.

Topfen Kuchen

CHEESECAKE

1 portion sweet shortcrust
    pastry (p. 145) for a 8½in
    spring-form pan
140g/⅔ cup sugar
75g/⅓ cup butter
1 tsp lemon zest
4 eggs, separated
50g/⅓ cup raisins
300g/1½ cups curds cheese,
    sieved
4 tbsp heavy cream

350°F for 1 hour

Par-bake a pastry case (p. 145) for 15 minutes. Leave to cool. Beat the sugar and butter until thick, pale and fluffy. Mix in the lemon zest and egg yolks, one at a time. Blend in the raisins and cheese. Beat the egg whites until they form peaks and fold them into the cheese mixture. Fold in the heavy cream. Pour the filling into the pastry case and bake in the warmed oven until well risen and golden. Cool in the pan on a wire rack. The cake will collapse and crack as it cools, which is typical of cheesecakes. Dredge with confectioners' sugar to serve.

The cake freezes successfully for up to 2 months. Defrost at room temperature for 3-4 hours.

Habsburger Torte

Hazelnut sponge
butter, sugar and flour
for the pan
100g/7 tbsp sugar
6 eggs, separated
2in/vanilla pod, split
100g/³/₄ cup plus 1 tbsp
unpeeled, ground hazelnuts
50g/¹/₂ cup toasted bread crumbs

Chocolate sponge
100g/1 cup sugar
5 eggs separated
100g/1 cup unpeeled, ground
hazelnuts
110g/4oz best dark, bittersweet
chocolate, melted and cooled
25g/¹/₄ cup toasted bread crumbs

Chocolate filling
140g/²/₃ cup unsalted butter
140g/1¹/₄ cups confectioners'
sugar, sifted
130g/4¹/₂oz dark bittersweet
chocolate, melted and cooled
3 tbsp dark rum or coffee
liqueur

Pistachio and almond filling
100g/¹/₂ cup unsalted butter
100g/1 cup confectioners'
sugar, sifted
1in vanilla pod, split
130g/²/₃ cup pistachios, ground
130g/¹/₂ cup ground almonds

3 tbsp apricot jam
1¹/₂ portions thick chocolate
icing (p. 157)
hazelnuts and pistachios to
decorate

350°F for 30 minutes

This is an elaborate cake that takes quite some time to prepare, but it is ideal for a special function or celebration. It slices perfectly into thin pieces without collapsing and will serve about 40 people.

The moist texture and unusual taste of the unpeeled hazelnuts are a perfect foil for the sweeter fillings. Make it 2-3 days ahead of time so that the flavors may develop.

Butter, line with wax paper and butter again two 10¹/₂in spring-form pans. Dust with a mixture of sugar and flour and shake off the excess.

Make the hazelnut sponge by beating the sugar and egg yolks until pale, thick and fluffy. Add the seeds of vanilla and blend well. Mix in the nuts and bread crumbs and combine well. Beat the egg whites until they are firm and lightly fold them into the mixture. Pour the batter into one of the pans, level it out and tap the pan sharply on the work-top to pop any bubbles of air. Bake and cool.

After about 15 minutes of cooking time has elapsed make the chocolate sponge. Follow the same method as above, but before beating the egg whites, beat the melted chocolate into the nut mixture. Proceed as before; bake and cool.

Chocolate filling Beat the butter and confectioners' sugar until pale and fluffy. Mix in the cooled chocolate and the rum or liqueur. Cover and chill.

Pistachio and almond filling Beat the butter and confectioners' sugar with the vanilla seeds until pale and fluffy. Mix in the nuts. Cover and chill.

Trim the cake sides, then split the hazelnut sponge in two and place the base on a wire rack. Reserve one-third of the chocolate filling for piping decoration later and smooth the remainder on the sponge. Cover with the chocolate cake layer. On sifted confectioners' sugar roll out the pistachio paste to fit the cake and lay it on top; sandwich with the remaining hazelnut layer.

Heat the apricot jam with 2 tbsp water and strain. Brush the slightly cooled jam on the sides and top of the cake. Prepare the chocolate icing and pour it straight over the top and down the sides of the cake, smoothing with a palette knife as necessary (p. 156). Avoid touching the top or it will lose its sheen. Leave to set.

Fit a pastry bag with a small, star-shaped nozzle and fill with the reserved chocolate cream. Pipe stars around the edge of the cake and in the middle. Stud with hazelnuts and pistachios to decorate.

GUGELHUPF *(T)*: HUNYADY
CHESTNUT TORTE *(R)*:
VANILLE KIPFERLN *and*
NONNEN BRETZERLN (C):
LINZERTORTE *(L)*: *This
selection of cakes is typical of
the fare that is offered for a
Viennese afternoon
'Kaffeejause'.*

Punschtorte

175g/6oz caster sugar
4 egg yolks
1 tsp orange zest
1 tsp lemon zest
60g/2¹/₂oz butter, melted and
    cooled
3 egg whites
85g/1¹/₂oz potato flour, sifted

Punsch syrup
50ml/2floz water
100g/3¹/₂oz granulated sugar
3 tbsp lemon juice, strained
3 tbsp orange juice, strained
4 tbsp dark rum

2 tbsp apricot jam, strained

punch icing (p. 157)

180°C/350°F/Gas 4 for 30
    minutes

Butter and line two 20cm/8in spring-form tins.

Beat the caster sugar and egg yolks until thick, pale and creamy. Beat in the citrus zests. Slowly pour on the butter while still beating, taking care to leave the creamy sediment in the bottom of the pan. Whisk the egg whites into firm peaks and lightly fold them into the mixture, in three stages, alternating with siftings of potato flour. Divide the mixture equally between the two baking tins. Bake until golden and shrinking slightly from the sides of the tin. Leave to cool on wire racks.

Meanwhile, prepare the syrup. Dissolve the sugar in the water over gentle heat and boil to a thread stage (p. 151), draw off the heat, stir in the lemon and orange juice, and finally the rum. Leave to cool.

As soon as the cake layers have cooled, prick them both all over with a fork and brush liberally with the rum syrup. Place one layer on a wire rack and spread the apricot jam all over, sandwich with the other cake layer.

Make the punch icing and pour it straight over the cake. Smooth the sides using a palette knife but avoid touching the top. While still warm decorate with small pieces of candied orange and lemon peel.

Leave to mature for a day before cutting.

Vanille Kipferln

VANILLA CRESCENTS

140g/4¹/₂oz plain flour, sifted
100g/3¹/₂oz unsalted butter,
    chilled
50g/2oz ground almonds
40g/1¹/₂oz caster sugar
vanilla flavoured, sifted icing
    sugar for dredging

150°C/300°F/Gas 2 for 30
    minutes

Makes 20 pieces

Sift the flour on to the work-top and cut in the cold butter. Blend together into a fine crumb texture and fork in the almonds and sugar. Knead into a smooth pastry. Pinch off walnut-sized pieces and roll each into a cylindrical rope with tapered ends; curve gently into a crescent or quarter-moon shape. Transfer to a buttered and floured baking sheet and bake in the warmed oven until lightly coloured.

Prepare a large sheet of grease-proof paper and dredge generously with vanilla icing sugar. Remove the crescents from the oven and leave to cool for 1-2 minutes. While they are still warm, lift the pastries one at a time, between two forks, and roll them in the icing sugar so that they are completely coated. Leave to cool on a clean sheet of grease-proof paper on a wire rack.

The crescents will keep fresh for several weeks stored in an air-tight tin.

Orangen Torte

Orange cream
4 egg yolks
100g/3½oz caster sugar
100ml/3½floz orange juice,
*   strained*
2 tbsp orange zest
165g/5½oz unsalted butter
125ml/4floz double cream

The Punschtorte may be adapted to have a strong orange flavour. Leave out the rum in the syrup and fill and cover the layers with orange cream.

Prepare the sponge as above and leave to cool. Make the syrup using 5 tbsp each of orange and lemon juice. Brush the cooled syrup over the cake layers.

Whisk the egg yolks, sugar, orange juice and zest in a heat-proof bowl. Set the bowl on a pan a quarter filled with simmering water and cook until the mixture has thickened, stirring all the time. Draw off the heat and beat until cool. Beat the butter separately until creamy, then beat the cool cream into it, a spoonful at a time. Whisk the double cream until it is stiff and gently fold into the main mixture. Chill before using.

Split the cake in half and spread one-third of the cream over the bottom layer. Sandwich with the top sponge layer. Smooth the rest of the cream round the sides and over the top of the cake. Decorate with slices of candied orange and lemon peel and angelica. Chill before serving.

Sachertorte

CHOCOLATE CAKE

140g/4½oz butter
110g/4oz caster sugar
4 egg yolks
175g/6oz plain, dessert
*   chocolate, melted and*
*   cooled*
1 tbsp vanilla sugar
2 drops bitter almond essence
75g/3oz plain flour, sifted
3 egg whites
apricot jam
thick chocolate icing (p. 157) or
*   chocolate fondant (p. 154)*

170°C/325°F/Gas 3 for 1 hour

Sachertorte was invented in Vienna in the mid-nineteenth century by the chef Franz Sacher for his employer Prince Lothar Metternich. In the 1880s Franz's youngest son, Edward, founded the famous Hotel Sacher in Vienna, which later, under the direction of his wife Frau Anna Sacher, became immensely popular and fashionable among the gentry and important people of the realm and the rendezvous for their entertaining and merry-making. The clientele flocked there to sample the excellent cuisine and, of course, the exclusive Sachertorte. The recipe was a secret and later became the subject of an acrimonious court case that lasted for seven years and was known as the 'Sweet Seven Years' War'.

What the magic ingredients are is still, however, a closely guarded secret. The recipe-books of the time give numerous variations: sometimes the cakes are filled and layered with apricot jam, some are made with almonds, other are based on equal-weight measures. Basically, it is a chocolate sponge cake, covered with apricot jam and a thick coating of dark, rich dessert chocolate.

Cream the butter with the sugar until pale and fluffy. Beat in the egg yolks, one at a time, and the cooled chocolate. Beat in the vanilla sugar and bitter almond essence and continue beating for 15 minutes by machine (25 minutes by hand). Sift the flour over the mixture and quickly but lightly blend it in without over-beating. Whisk the egg whites until they stand in stiff, creamy peaks and fold them into the mixture. Pour it into a buttered 24cm/9½in spring-form tin — the mixture should be no more than 4cm/1¼in deep. Bake in the warmed oven until slightly shrinking from the sides of the tin. Cool on a wire rack.

Brush the cake with strained apricot jam and glaze with the chocolate icing.

HUNGARY

Dobostorta Poppy Seed or Walnut Roll Hunyady Chestnut Torta
Curds Cheese Cake Switzen Plum Tart
Morello Cherry Tart with Sour-cream Pastry
Strudel, Rètes and Fila Doughs Curds Cheese Strudel
Apple Strudel Lemon and Almond Strudel Russian Cream Cake
Hazelnut Torta Acacia Honey Cake

Dobostorta

DRUM CAKE

Sponge
6 egg yolks
130g/½ cup sugar
1 tsp orange zest
65g/½ cup plus 1 tbsp all-
    purpose flour
65g/5 tbsp potato flour
6 egg whites

1 portion cooked buttercream
    with egg yolks (p. 150)
    flavored with chocolate and
    rum

Caramel glaze
165g/⅔ cup sugar

350°F for 5-8 minutes for each
    layer

Beat the egg yolks and sugar until pale and creamy. Mix in the orange zest. Sift together both the flours to aerate well and add to the egg yolks. Beat the egg whites in a separate bowl until they are firm and well peaked. Fold the egg snow into the yolk mixture lightly and quickly.

This quantity makes six layers. Spread a thin coating of mixture in the bottom of a greased and floured 9½in spring-form pan and smooth carefully. Bake immediately in the preheated oven. (Bake two layers at a time if you have the pans.) When it is colored light gold, remove the cake from the oven and turn out of the pan straight on to a wire rack to cool. Make the remaining layers in the same way.

Assemble the cake as soon as the layers have cooled so that they do not dry out and become crisp.

Set aside the best-looking cake layer and sandwich the rest together with chocolate filling, spreading it over the top and the sides.

Prepare the top layer. Brush any loose crumbs off the cake and lay it on a large sheet of wax paper. Take two long knives, lightly greasing the blade of one with oil or butter.

Make the caramel glaze by gently heating 65g/⅓ cup sugar in a heavy pan until golden, then add the rest of the sugar and cook until it has thickened. Quickly pour the caramel straight over the cake layer and smooth it out using the clean knife. Using the greased knife, immediately mark the cake out into 10 sections and cut through the sugar glaze. Leave to cool. Lay the caramel disc on top of the filled cake layers.

Do not store in the refrigerator as this spoils the caramel surface.

DOBOSTORTA: *Here the caramel was poured onto wax paper and cut into triangles. They were then embedded in the chocolate filling, slightly at an angle to create a fan effect.*

CURDS CHEESE CAKE: *This has a very fine mousse-like texture and rises quite spectacularly as it bakes — then drops: do not hesitate to push it back into the pan while it is cooling.*

Poppy Seed or Walnut Roll

Yeast pastry

75ml/¹/₃ cup milk
25g/1oz fresh yeast
500g/4 cups bread flour, sifted
100g/¹/₂ cup sugar
pinch salt
225g/1 cup butter
2 egg yolks
50ml/¹/₄ cup dairy sour cream
1 whole egg for brushing

Poppy seed filling

100ml/7 tbsp milk
*200g/1³/₄ cups poppy seeds,
    ground*
140g/²/₃ cup sugar
2 tsp grated lemon zest
*1 large dessert apple, peeled
    and grated*

Walnut filling

140g/²/₃ cup sugar
3 tbsp milk
200g/1³/₄ cups ground walnuts
1 tsp grated lemon zest
*2 dessert apples, peeled and
    grated*

350°F for 1 hour

Makes 2 rolls

This yeasted roll is served all the year round in Hungary as a coffee-time pastry.

Prepare a sponge batter (p. 149). Warm the milk to blood heat and sprinkle over the crumbled yeast; mix in 100g/¹/₃ cup flour taken from the recipe and 1 tsp sugar. Beat well. Cover and leave to rise until at least double in bulk. Meanwhile, sift the flour and salt into a large bowl, cut in the butter and rub to a crumb texture. Mix in the sugar and egg yolks, then pour on the sponge batter. Beat in enough sour cream to make a not too soft dough. Knead thoroughly until the dough becomes elastic and throws large air bubbles. Leave in the bowl closely covered with a cloth, or place the dough in a large, lightly oiled plastic bag and seal. Set in a warm place to rise for about 3 hours until it has at least doubled in bulk.

While the dough is rising make the filling.

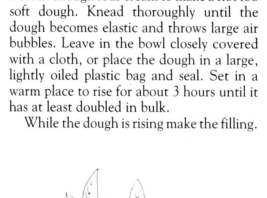

Poppy seed filling   Boil the milk and pour it over the ground poppy seeds; leave to infuse and swell. Gently dissolve the sugar in 2 tbsp water, sieve the seed and stir into the syrup; draw off the heat. Stir in the lemon zest and grated apple. Cool before using.

Walnut filling   Dissolve the sugar in the milk to make a syrup. Stir in the walnuts, and draw off the heat. Mix in the lemon zest and grated apple. Cool before using.

For a very simple filling sprinkle a mixture of 140g/²/₃ sugar, 2 tsp ground cinnamon and ¹/₂ tsp ground cloves over the dough before rolling it up.

Turn the risen dough on to a floured pastry board, knock it back for a moment or two, then divide it into two, replacing the unused piece in the covered bowl or bag.

Roll out the dough into a rectangle ¹/₄in thick. Spread generously with the chosen filling to within ³/₄in of the edge and roll up carefully, tucking in both ends so that the filling cannot leak out. Transfer the roll to a lightly greased baking sheet, with the open seam underneath. Brush lightly with beaten egg and leave to rise for a further 30 minutes. Brush again with beaten egg and prick all over with a fork. Bake in a preheated oven. Finish the reserve dough in the same way.

Serve cut in slices. They keep well at least a week in a covered container.

Curds Cheese Cake

130g/1 cup plus 1½ tbsp all-
  purpose flour
65g/5 tbsp butter
1 tsp sugar
1 egg yolk
140ml/⅔ cup dairy sour cream
confectioners' sugar for
  dredging

Filling
7 egg yolks
250g/1 cup plus 2 tbsp sugar
2 tbsp lemon zest
270g/1¼ cups curds cheese
8 egg whites

325°F for 50-60 minutes

Curds cheese, like sour cream, is an important ingredient in Hungarian cooking. The airy, mousse-like filling of this cake has a lemony tang, which is enchanced by the sour cream pastry.

Sift the flour into a bowl and drop in the butter, cut in pieces. Rub together to make fine crumbs. Mix in the sugar. Add the egg and sour cream and blend and knead into a firm paste. Roll into a ball, wrap in plastic wrap and chill for 30 minutes.

Divide the dough in two and roll out each piece to fit a 10½in spring-form pan. Line the greased base of the pan with one sheet of pastry. Make pastry leaves or flowers with any remaining scraps of dough.

Beat together the egg yolks and sugar until pale and creamy and well expanded. Beat in the lemon zest and the sieved cheese. In another bowl beat up the egg whites until they are firm and well peaked. Lightly fold them into the cheese mixture using a large metal spoon and taking care not to lose any air. Pour the filling into the cake pan. Smooth gently, then lay the remaining sheet of pastry on top and press it down lightly. Place pastry leaves or flowers quickly on the pastry top, using a little beaten egg white. Bake immediately in the preheated oven. The cake will color only slightly and rise quite high out of the tin. As it cools it will drop quite dramatically — most cheesecakes do — but it will not crack because of the pastry covering. Dredge with confectioners' sugar to serve.

Acacia Honey Cake

320ml/1 cup acacia honey
3 whole eggs, lightly beaten
300g/2¾ cups rye flour
1 tsp ground cinnamon
large pinch crushed cloves
110/1½ cup coarse, ground
  unblanched almonds or
  hazelnuts
2 tbsp dark rum
½ tsp baking soda
blanched almond halves to
  decorate

350°F for 30-35 minutes

Honey cakes are among the earliest to be found throughout the world. They were usually prepared for festivals and celebrations, and later, as life became more sophisticated, they were baked in elaborately carved, wooden or metal molds depicting the appropriate occasion. Though the ingredients were much the same — rye flour, spices, candied fruits and nuts — the honey of the region lent its own distinctive character to the flavor of the cake. In Hungary, acacia blossom perfumes the pale, clear lemon-colored honey, and this imparts a slightly bitter-sweet taste.

Warm the honey in the jar set in a pan of hot water, then pour it into a large mixing bowl and beat until it is frothy, thick and white. Beat in the eggs and add the flour a spoonful at a time. Mix together the spices and ground nuts and stir in the rum, and combine with the honey and egg mixture. Dissolve the baking soda with the milk and beat it into the mixture. Leave to mature in a covered bowl overnight as this helps to lighten the mixture.

Press the paste into a greased and floured deep rectangular baking pan 12½ × 8½in. Stud with almond halves and bake. Avoid letting it brown too much as this gives a bitter taste. When the cake has cooled in the pan, cut it into rectangular pieces and store for at least a week in an air-tight container before serving.

MORELLO CHERRY TART:
*A simple tea-time dessert
that is not too sweet.*

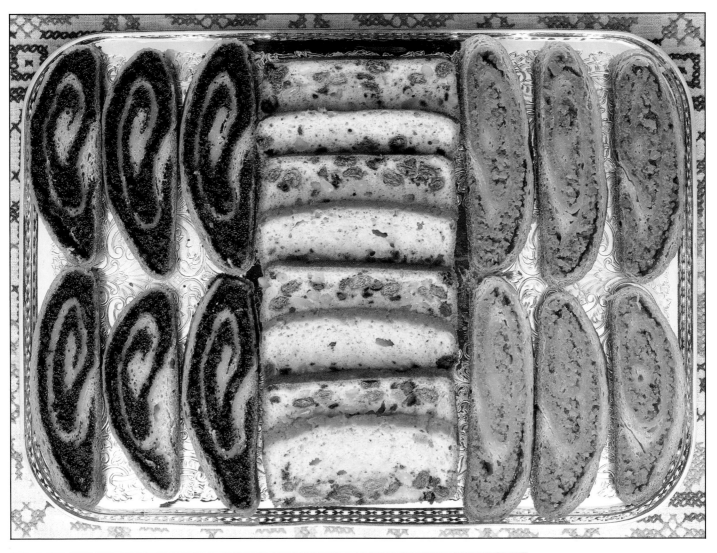

POPPY SEED AND WALNUT ROLL *and* BISCHOFBROD: *The dried fruit and nut slices of Bischofbrod in the picture also taste good spread with butter. Yeasted walnut and poppy seed rolls hold a better round shape if they are loosely wrapped in wax paper before being baked.*

ACACIA HONEY CAKE: *Honey cakes are among the oldest cakes in history and were usually served for festive occasions. Honey was in use as a sweetener long before sugar was discovered.*

Hazelnut Torte

4 egg yolks
140g/²/₃ cup sugar
140g/1 cup ground, toasted
    hazelnuts
1 tbsp toasted bread crumbs
1¹/₂ tbsp dark rum
3 egg whites
butter and flour for the pan

350°F for 1 hour

Almonds or walnuts may be substituted in this basic recipe.

Beat the egg yolks and 100g/¹/₂ cup sugar until pale and creamy. Beat in the nuts, bread crumbs and rum. Beat the egg whites in a separate bowl until they stand in firm, snowy peaks. Beat in the rest of the sugar. Lightly fold the egg snow into the main mixture in three stages, taking care not to stir it and break down the pockets of air. Pour the mixture into a greased and floured 8¹/₂in spring-form pan and bake in the pre-heated oven until well risen and brown. Leave in the pan for 10 minutes before turning out on to a wire rack to finish cooling.

The cake may be dressed up in several ways. Dredge it with confectioners' sugar and offer whipped cream on the side. Glaze it with rum icing decorated with whole caramelized nuts (p. 9). It can also be divided into three layers and filled with strained apricot jam and a layer of whipped cream, then finished with chocolate icing. A chocolate cream filling is especially good: use half a portion of the basic buttercream (p. 150) flavored with 1 tbsp instant coffee and 1 tbsp coffee liqueur. Chill overnight before cutting. Dredge with confectioners' sugar to serve.

Hunyady Chestnut Torta

75g/3oz finest dark,
    bittersweet chocolate
1 tbsp rum
130g/²/₃ cup sugar
4 eggs, separated
350g/12oz chestnuts, shelled,
    cooked and sieved
2 tbsp potato flour
butter and flour for the pan

Hazelnut filling

75g/²/₃ cup toasted hazelnuts,
    ground
3 egg yolks
75g/¹/₃ cup unsalted butter
75g/³/₄ cup confectioners' sugar
2 tbsp coffee liqueur or rum

apricot jam, strained
thick chocolate icing (p. 157) or
    140ml/²/₃ cup heavy or
    whipping cream, whipped
2 tbsp sugar
2 tbsp coffee liqueur or rum

350°F for 50 minutes

Carefully melt the chocolate in 1 tbsp water and stir in the rum. Leave to cool. Beat together the sugar and egg yolks until pale and creamy. Beat in the chocolate and stir in the sieved chestnuts. Beat the egg whites in a separate bowl, until they hold firm peaks, and lightly fold them into the chestnut mixture using a large metal spoon. Sift over and fold in the potato flour. Grease and wax paper line two 8¹/₂in greased and floured spring-form pans and bake until well risen, leave to cool in the pans before turning out on to wire racks. Strip off the papers carefully.

To make the filling, mix the hazelnuts and one egg yolk to a smooth paste. Cream the butter and sugar until light and fluffy and beat in the remaining egg yolks one at a time. Mix in the hazelnut paste and liqueur or rum. Chill.

Split both sponge layers in two and fill with the hazelnut cream. Sandwich both cakes with 2 tbsp strained and warmed apricot jam. Cover the cake and leave to chill for a day.

Brush the top and sides of the cake with warmed, strained apricot jam. Make the icing (p. 157). Pour the warm icing straight over the cake, smooth out and decorate. Do not leave the cake in a cold place as it will spoil the gloss of the icing.

For a *whipped cream filling* sweeten the cream with the sugar and blend in 2 tbsp rum or coffee liqueur. Sandwich the two cakes with cream, reserving some for the top and sides. Smooth the rest of the cream all over the cake and decorate with candied chestnut pieces, toasted hazelnuts and chocolate curls. This should be assembled 3-4 hours before it is to be eaten.

Switzen Plum Tart

65g/1⅓ cup all-purpose flour
100g/7 tbsp butter, cut in pieces
1 tbsp sugar
1 egg yolk
pinch salt
1 tbsp dairy sour cream
1 tbsp toasted bread crumbs
2 tsp ground cinnamon
500g/1lb Switzen plums,
　　stoned
2 tbsp sugar for dredging

Top
1 egg yolk
40g/3 tbsp sugar
75ml/⅓ cup dairy sour cream
2 egg whites
25g/3 tbsp all-purpose flour

350°F for 1 hour

Once again sour cream is the basis of this distinctive light, almost flaky, pastry. This plum tart and the recipe that follows are very typical but quite different from each other, one filled with morello cherries and the other with Switzen plums. If morello cherries are unavailable, bitter or well-flavored dark cherries will do. Switzen plums usually appear in mid-autumn. They have deep purple skins and firm green flesh, and their slightly tart taste blends exceptionally well with the sweet-and-sour pastry. No other plum will really replace them, but if you cannot obtain them, be sure to choose a variety that has a good strong flavor.

Combine the flour with the butter pieces and rub to a fine crumb texture. Toss in the sugar. Mix in the egg yolk, salt, and enough sour cream to blend it all to a firm smooth paste. Roll into a ball, wrap in plastic film and chill in the refrigerator for 1 hour. Roll out the pastry and line the base of a 9½in spring-form pan. Prick all over with a fork. Scatter the mixture of bread crumbs and cinnamon on the pastry and cover with a close layer of plums. Dredge with the sugar.

To prepare the top beat the egg yolk and half the sugar until creamy and pale, and mix in the sour cream. Beat the egg whites until firm, then beat in the rest of the sugar until the mixture is satiny and smooth. Fold the egg snow and spoonfuls of sifted flour alternately into the main mixture. Spoon over the top of the plums and level out. Bake until well risen and golden.

Dredge with confectioners' sugar to serve and eat either warm or cold.

Morello Cherry Tart

175g/1½ cups all-purpose flour
　　pinch salt
65g/5 tbsp butter, cut in pieces
2 tsp sugar
1 egg yolk
50ml/¼ cup dairy sour cream
2 tbsp toasted bread crumbs
700g/1½lb fresh or bottled
　　morello cherries
75g/¾ cup ground walnuts
1 tsp grated lemon zest
2 tbsp vanilla sugar
50g/¼ cup sugar
1 egg white, lightly beaten
2 tbsp walnuts, chopped
whipped cream to serve

350°F for 1 hour

Prepare the pastry and chill it overnight in the refrigerator.

Sift the flour and salt into a bowl, drop in the butter pieces and blend to a crumb texture. Mix in the sugar. Add the egg yolk and enough sour cream to make a firm paste. Knead well, divide in two and wrap in plastic wrap. Chill. Roll out each piece large enough to fit a 9½in spring-form pan. Line the base and sides of the pan with wax paper, grease well and lay a sheet of pastry on the bottom; scatter over half the bread crumbs.

Wash and dry the cherries and remove the stones. If using bottled fruit, drain well and dry on paper towels. Mix the fruit in the bowl with the ground walnuts, lemon zest and vanilla sugar, and spread the mixture on the bread crumb base in the tin. Sprinkle with the rest of the bread crumbs and the sugar and cover with the remaining piece of pastry. Brush with egg white and scatter the chopped walnuts all over the top. Bake in the preheated oven until slightly colored. Serve either warm or cold, with whipped cream on the side.

Strudel, Rètes and Fila Doughs

Strudel, rètes and fila are basically the same dough, and although both Austria and Hungary lay claim to its origins, the Middle East must really take the credit. The well-kneaded dough is very elastic and can be stretched out until it is paper-thin; it then bakes into golden-brown, feather-like, crisp layers.

Fila pastry is usually made with flour and water, and butter is brushed between the sheets of pastry later, as it is assembled in layers. Traditionally it is rolled and folded into small parcels, shaped as triangles, snails, envelopes and cigars, or layered in a tray with a filling and cut into lozenge shapes. Savory fillings consist of meat, vegetables and cheeses, and the sweet variations, generally almonds and pistachios or curds cheese, are often bathed in a perfumed sugar syrup flavored with rose or orange-flower water.

The same technique is used to prepare strudel and rètes dough, but oil or butter enriches the basic ingredients, and a single finished sheet is rolled around the filling to form a large, flattened cylindrical roll. The selection of filling ingredients is much more unusual, however: cabbage, potato and almonds, semolina, poppy seeds, herbs, and ham or crab may be used as well as the sweet fillings with which we are much more familiar — apples, cherries and plums and nuts, curds cheese and dried fruits.

When making strudel dough use bread flour, which is high in gluten and gives greater elasticity to the dough making it easier to handle.

Both strudel and fila pastries may be bought ready-made.

Strudel and rètes pastry

2 tbsp butter or 3 tbsp
 vegetable oil plus extra for
 brushing
200ml/³/₄ cup plus 1 tbsp water
300g/2¼ cups bread flour
pinch salt
1 egg

Place the butter or oil and water in a small pan and heat gently until the butter has melted. Set aside.

Sift the flour and salt two or three times and finally on to a pastry board. Make a well in the center, drop in the egg and the luke-warm butter water. Blend in the flour and knead gently at first, for the dough will be rather sticky, but continue kneading until it comes cleanly off the fingers and the board. Wash your hands in between and dust with more flour if necessary. Continue working and kneading the dough for about 15 minutes until it is smooth and elastic and air bubbles start to develop. Roll it into a ball, place on a freshly floured corner of the board and brush with melted butter. Cover with a warm bowl and leave to rest for 15-20 minutes.

It is simplest to roll out and stretch the dough on a table so that you can work round all the sides.

Cover the table with a large, clean cloth dusted heavily with flour. Place the dough in the center, pat it into a square and roll it out thinly. Brush with more melted butter if it starts to dry out.

Now the dough is pulled and stretched by hand. Flour your hands and place them under the pastry, backs uppermost and thumbs tucked out of the way. If two people can work, so much the better, otherwise lay the rolling pin on the other end of the pastry to stop it slipping. Working from the middle outwards, gently pull the pastry and stretch it evenly until it is paper-thin and almost transparent. Gently drop the dough down on the floured cloth, move around and start working on the next side; continue until the whole piece of pastry is evenly stretched. Cut away the thicker edges. Leave to dry for a few minutes, then brush with melted butter before filling.

Fila dough

Fila pastry is a good alternative to strudel and may be bought in Greek and Middle Eastern shops.

Fila dries out very quickly when it is exposed to air, so you have work fast once you begin preparation. Have the filling prepared, the butter ready-melted and work with only half a package at a time. Fila may be stored in the freezer for up to 2 months; after that it crumbles and disintegrates when it is defrosted.

500g/1lb or 12 sheets fila pastry will require 225g/1 cup melted, unsalted butter.

Dust a clean dish towel with flour. Lay a sheet of fila pastry on it and brush all over with melted butter. Cover with another sheet of pastry and brush this with butter too. Continue layering and brushing with butter in this way until all the sheets are used.

Place the filling on the pastry and roll it up, tucking in the sides so that the filling cannot escape. Transfer to a greased baking sheet, seam side down, and brush with melted butter and bake as for strudel.

LEMON AND ALMOND STRUDEL *and* APPLE STRUDEL: *These are at their best when eaten warm. They are made with fila dough, which is very popular in Middle Eastern cuisine.*

RUSSIAN CREAM CAKE: *Nuts make an interesting alternative to the fruits in this cake — try walnuts, hazelnuts and almonds with the candied peel and golden raisins.*

Curds Cheese Strudel

Filling

50g/¹/₂ cup golden raisins
1 tbsp rum
110g/¹/₂ cup butter, softened
75g/¹/₃ cup sugar
4 egg yolks
300g/1¹/₄ cup curds cheese,
*   sieved*
50ml/¹/₄ cup dairy sour cream
1 tsp lemon zest
confectioners' sugar for
*   dredging*

1 portion strudel dough (p. 82)
*   or 12 sheets of fila pastry*
melted butter for brushing

400°F for 30 minutes

Soak the raisins in the rum for 30 minutes to plump. Beat the butter and sugar until light and fluffy. Beat in the egg yolks one at a time. Mix in the cheese, sour cream and zest. Spread the filling over two-thirds of the pastry and sprinkle with raisins and rum. Then using the cloth to help, roll the pastry loosely over the filling; tuck in the ends carefully, so that the filling cannot leak out, and transfer to a large, greased baking sheet, seam side down. Brush with more melted butter and bake in the preheated oven for about 30 minutes until crisp and well browned. Serve warm or cold dredged with confectioners' sugar.

If using fila pastry, use six sheets at a time. Brush one sheet with melted unsalted butter and cover with a second sheet of pastry; brush with more melted butter and continue layering and brushing with butter with the remaining layers. Place half the cheese filling in the middle and roll up in the same way as for strudel. Finish with the rest of the fila sheets in the same way.

Lemon and Almond Strudel

Filling

50g/¹/₃ cup butter
2 egg yolks
1 whole egg
100g/¹/₂ cup sugar
grated zest of 2 lemons
1¹/₂ tbsp lemon juice, strained
50g/¹/₄ cup sugar
2 egg whites
melted butter for brushing
75g/¹/₃ cup ground almonds

1 portion strudel dough (p. 82)
*   or 12 sheets of fila pastry*

400°F for 30 minutes

Beat the butter until pale and creamy. Beat in the egg yolks one at a time and the whole egg. Beat in the 100g/¹/₂ cup sugar and mix in the lemon zest. Set aside. Beat together the lemon juice and 50g/¹/₄ cup sugar. Beat the egg whites until they stand in firm, snowy peaks and beat the lemon juice and sugar mixture into them until they are thick and glossy. Brush the strudel dough with melted butter and cover two-thirds with the butter and egg yolk filling. Scatter the ground almonds all over and cover with the lemon and egg white mixture. Roll up the strudel lightly. Brush with melted butter and finish as before.

Walnut and poppy seed fillings (p. 76) also taste good with strudel pastry.

Apple Strudel

Lightly toast 100g/1 cup bread crumbs in 100g/$\frac{1}{2}$ cup butter and leave to cool. Peel core and slice about 1 kilo/2lb well-flavored, dessert apples into $\frac{1}{4}$ slices. Scatter the crumbs over the pastry to insulate it from the fruit. Cover with the apple slices and dredge with a mixture of 100g/$\frac{1}{2}$ cup sugar and 2 tsp ground cinnamon. Scatter over 100g/$\frac{3}{4}$ cup raisins that have been soaked in 1 tbsp rum, and splash the remaining rum on top. Roll up, brush with melted butter and finish as above. Bake. Dredge generously with confectioners' sugar to serve.

Cherries or Switzen plums are also suitable, and apricots quite delicious. Insulate the pastry base with ground walnuts or hazelnuts, using 85g/$\frac{3}{4}$ cup nuts and 25g/3 tbsp bread crumbs. Wash and stone the fruits beforehand.

Try an autumn mixture of fruits such as pears, apples, plums, blackberries and melon slices on a bed of fried and toasted bread crumbs; dredge with 125g/$\frac{1}{2}$ cup sugar.

400°F for 40 minutes

Russian Cream Cake

4 eggs, separated
75g/$\frac{1}{3}$ cup sugar
1 tsp orange zest
50g/$\frac{1}{2}$ cup all-purpose flour
50g/$\frac{1}{4}$ cup potato flour

Filling
25g/1$\frac{1}{2}$ tbsp chopped candied
   orange and lemon peel
25g/$\frac{1}{4}$ cup golden raisins
110g/$\frac{2}{3}$ cup glacé
   cherries, pineapple, plum,
   pear, angelica, etc
1$\frac{1}{2}$ tbsp dark rum
100ml/$\frac{1}{2}$ cup milk
vanilla pod
50g/$\frac{1}{4}$ cup sugar
3 egg yolks
1 tbsp gelatine powder
140ml/$\frac{2}{3}$ cup heavy cream

fruits for decoration

350°F for 40 minutes

To make the sponge beat the egg whites in a large, clean bowl, until they stand in firm, snowy peaks. Gradually sift and beat in the sugar until the mixture is satiny and smooth; mix in the zest. Lightly beat the egg yolks separately, then beat them into the meringue a spoonful at a time and continue to blend them in well. Sift over one-third of the flours and gently fold them in using a large metal spoon; fold in the rest of the flour in two stages. Pour the mixture into a greased and floured 8$\frac{1}{2}$in spring-form pan and bake until well risen and golden. Cool on a wire rack.

Meanwhile make the filling. Steep the candied peels, raisins and candied fruits in a bowl with the rum for 1 hour, mixing it every now and then. Bring the milk to the boil with a split piece of vanilla pod, draw off the heat and leave to infuse and cool. Remove the pod. Beat together the sugar and the egg yolks in a heat-proof bowl, sprinkle over the gelatine powder and gradually pour on the cooled milk, beating all the time. Place the

bowl over a pan, a quarter filled with simmering water, and stir gently while the custard cooks and thickens. Set aside to cool.

Beat the cream until softly peaked. Beat the vanilla custard until smooth and creamy, then fold it into the whipped cream together with the soaked fruits and rum. Leave to chill for 1 hour.

Cut the sponge into three layers. Reserve about one-third of the cream for the top and the sides of the cake and use the rest to fill the two layers. Cover the top and sides of cake with the rest of the cream, then decorate with pieces of fruit. Chill for 3-4 hours before serving.

GERMANY

*Sandtorte Black Forest Kirschtorte Baumkuchen
Zwetschkenkuchen Käsekuchen Streusselkuchen
Frankfurter Kranz Bienenstich Apfelkuchen Schraderpuffer
Lebkuchen Mohrenkopf*

The cooking of the monks in the monastery kitchens was an important early influence in both Switzerland and Germany, which was then no more than a jumble of small principalities, feudal bishoprics and free cities. The Monks kept bees, and honey was used for sweetening long before sugar was available. Honey and spiced cakes had been traditional fare for pagan feasts from early times, but the monks introduced them to the more northerly countries. Nuremberg, situated in the middle of the German lands, became one of the principal trading towns along the north/south route, and by the fourteenth century it had developed into a thriving centre. Traders brought pepper, ginger, cinnamon, nutmeg, aniseed, almonds, rose water, citron and orange with them, and, when these were combined with the local honey, a new exciting *Kuchen* was invented. A specialist Guild was formed to exploit the advantages of this new *Lebkuchen*, and it became such a popular speciality that two centuries later a Christmas market specializing in the sale was established and still exists today.

In later times specialist shops sold wooden *Lebkuchen* and *spekulatius* molds, which had a variety of both secular and religious themes carved on them. Housewives also enjoyed coloring the baked pastries, using natural dyes in the icings. Egg yolk and saffron gave a strong yellow tint; parsley and spinach, green; black came from blood; red from Turnsole (red orchil), brown from cinnamon and blue from violets but in Frankfurt in 1791 the coloring of foods was however forbidden for health reasons.

Apart from monastic influences, the differences between the early cuisine of the poor and that of the princely courts and dukedoms was marked. The prosperous gentry employed skilled kitchen staff and provided elaborate kitchens and sophisticated equipment. The choice of ingredients was extensive and, with more refined techniques, the bakers could produce finer and lighter sponge and pound cakes, which were more suited to the spoiled palates of their employers.

Christmas cakes, other than *Lebkuchen* which were quite different, were *Stollen* and *Striezel*. These yeasted loaves, enriched with nuts and dried fruits, varied from region to region, but *Stollen*, representing Christ wrapped in swaddling clothes, and *Striezel*, a simple heavy plait, remain the traditional shapes.

Yeast baking tended to be more popular among the lower classes, for yeast cakes were more economical, needing little sweetening, and fresh cherries, plums, apples and cream cheese tasted good on the plain dough. A simple hearth oven with a good strong fire was probably sufficient to bake the dough adequately, although housewives would often simply take their own enriching nuts, spices and fruits to the village baker, who would provide the bread dough and bake it in his bread oven.

As closed cooking ranges improved and became more generally available, baking

A confectioner's dream — with cookie production in full swing. Each person has their own particular job so that they soon become quite specialized and very speedy.

Honey was used as a sweetener in early times and bee-keeping was a prime responsibility of the monks. Their spiced honey cakes were especially popular for religious festivals.

in the home in the late eighteenth and nineteenth centuries increased in popularity. At about the same time the price of sugar fell dramatically, stimulating a great enthusiasm for cake-baking in particular.

A north German cookery book, written in 1842 by Henrietta Davidis, included 134 recipes for *Torten* and *Kuchen* and 116 for small pastries and filled cakes. In contrast, Eliza Acton's *Modern Cookery for Private Families*, published in England in 1845, included only the plainest of cakes such as madeira, pound and gingerbread, a few cookies and some sweet and savory pastries. She really did not approve of sweet cakes at all.

A decade later in Germany cakes were served as a meal, along with a few savouries, as an accompaniment to coffee or tea on the *Kaffeetisch* and in the *Konditorei*. Here lay the gugelhopf, spiced honey cakes, yeast breads and pastries of Switzerland, Austria and Hungary; the meringues and choux pastry confections of France; fruit cakes from England; macaroons from Italy. The housewife was judged by the baked cakes on her table, and *Gemütlichkeit* was the essence of her hospitality.

In Germany today the selection of cakes and pastries is still as varied as in the past and the finest quality — the traditional *Kaffeetisch* lives on.

This smiling country girl is obviously enjoying her simple task.

BLACK FOREST KIRSCH
TORTE: *Chocolate and*
cherries, nuts, whipped
cream and kirsch make this
the most tempting and
luscious after-dinner dessert.

Sandtorte

SANDCAKE

165g/²/₃ cup butter
165g/²/₃ cup sugar
1 egg
3 egg yolks
1 tbsp rum
¹/₂ tsp lemon zest
¹/₄ tsp baking powder
165g/²/₃ cup potato flour,
    sifted
2 egg whites
confectioners' sugar for
    dredging

325°F for 1 hour

Sandtorte is related to pound cake (p. 41), but the method of preparation is quite different. The mixture has to be beaten for a considerable time so that when it has been baked the texture is fine and sand-like. Potato flour gives added refinement with a powdery dense texture and a sweet, nutty flavor.

Gently melt the butter in a small pan, taking care not to let it brown. As it starts to bubble, draw the pan off the heat and carefully pour the clear liquid into a small mixing bowl, leaving the thick sediment in the bottom of the pan. Allow to cool. As it starts to solidify, set the bowl on a bed of ice cubes and beat the clarified butter for 10 minutes by machine (20 minutes by hand) until it is very thick and almost white. Transfer the butter to a large bowl. Add the sugar, egg and egg yolks a little at a time, making sure that the mixture never becomes runny, and beat for a further 15 minutes. Slowly add the rum, beating all the time, then the zest. Sift the flour and baking powder and fold in half but do not over-blend. Beat the egg whites until they are stiff and fold them into the main mixture in three stages, alternating with siftings of flour. Pour into a greased and floured 1 kg/9 × 5 × 3in (2qt) loaf pan and smooth out. Bake in the preheated oven. Turn out of the pan to cool on a wire rack. Dredge with confectioners' sugar to serve. Keeps fresh for up to a week.

Apfelkuchen

APPLE SPONGE

110g/¹/₂ cup sugar
110g/¹/₂ cup butter
2 eggs
2 tbsp milk
175g/1¹/₂ cups all-purpose flour
1 tsp baking powder
500g/1lb cooking apples, cut
    into ¹/₄in slices
2 tbsp sugar for dredging
whipped cream to serve

350°F for 1 hour

Beat the sugar and butter until pale and fluffy. Beat in the eggs one at a time and the milk and blend well. Sift the flour with the baking powder to aerate well, then combine lightly with the main mixture without over-beating. Pour the mixture into a 8in spring-form pan, greased and lined with wax paper, and smooth the top. Press the prepared apples into the surface of the mixture in an even pattern.

Bake in the preheated oven until well risen and golden. Test for readiness. Lift the tin out of the oven and dredge the surface with sugar. Remove the cake from the tin, peel off the paper and leave to cool on a wire rack.

Serve warm as a pudding or cold with whipped cream on the side.

Black Forest Kirschtorte

butter, flour and sugar for the
  pan
75g/³/₄ cup unblanched
  almonds, coarsely ground
50g/¹/₂ cup toasted bread
  crumbs
1 tsp ground cinnamon
1 tsp ground cloves
2 tbsp kirsch
130g/¹/₂ cup plus 1 tbsp sugar
9 egg yolks
2 tsp orange zest
100g/3¹/₂oz bittersweet dessert
  chocolate, melted and
  cooled
6 egg whites

Filling
1 kg/2lb morello, sour or black
  cherries, washed and stoned
  or 850g/1lb 12oz canned
  pitted cherries
250ml/1 cup red wine
250ml/1¹/₄ cups water
100g/¹/₂ cup sugar
cinnamon stick
2 tsp grated orange zest
140ml/²/₃ cup kirsch
425ml/2 cups heavy or
  whipping cream
3 tbsp sugar
4 tbsp grated chocolate and
  chocolate curls and
  confectioners' sugar for
  decoration

350°F for 30 minutes

Black cherries combined with chocolate or nuts in cakes were very popular in south Germany, Austria and Switzerland during the last century. Occasionally the cakes were built in layers, but mostly a layer of fresh fruit was covered with the uncooked cake mixture or blended with it and, typical of those regions, nuts were often included. Kirsch was not evident although rum was very common.

Kirsch was distilled and drunk during the 1800s but seems rarely to have been used as a flavoring in cakes until this century. A 1928 edition of an extremely popular southern German cookery book, instructs that *Kirschgeist* (spirit) be used to soak with fruits in a *Topf* (pot). When the chocolate and cherry kirsch torte was actually created has been difficult to establish, but undoubtedly the sharp and potent cherry taste gives a spirited and cleansing kick to what might otherwise be a rather sweet and sickly confection.

Today there is still no traditional recipe for Black Forest Kirschtorte. It may be made with layers of plain chocolate sponge with or without butter and including nuts, but common to all are cherries, chocolate, cream and kirsch, and this tempting combination entices so many people that it is probably the youngest but most popular traditional cake in the world today.

Prepare two 8¹/₂in spring-form pans: butter, line the base with wax paper, butter again, dredge with sugar and flour. Mix together the almonds, bread crumbs, cinnamon and cloves and moisten with kirsch.

In a separate bowl beat the sugar and egg yolks until thick, pale and creamy. Mix in the orange zest and chocolate. Lightly combine with the first mixture. Beat the egg whites separately until they hold firm snowy peaks. Lightly and quickly fold them into the main mixture until just combined.

Divide the mixture equally between the two pans. Smooth the top and tap each tin once to disperse any air pockets. Bake in the preheated oven until well risen and slightly shrinking away from the sides of the pans. Cool on wire racks.

To cook the fresh cherries for the filling, combine the wine, water and sugar in a pan and heat gently until the sugar has dissolved. Add the cinnamon stick and orange zest, and simmer for about 20 minutes. Drop in the cleaned fruits and poach lightly for 10 minutes. Lift the fruits carefully out of the syrup and drain in a colander. Boil the syrup on a high heat for two minutes to reduce and thicken it slightly. Draw off the heat and leave to cool.

Mix 75ml/¹/₃ cup of cherry syrup with 125ml/¹/₂ cup kirsch. Dry the cherries with absorbent paper towels. Beat the cream until softly peaked and beat in the sugar until firm; fold in the remaining kirsch. Cut both chocolate sponges across the middle. Reserve 3-4 tbsp cream and a few cherries for decoration.

Place a sponge base on an elegant serving plattter and sprinkle over about one-third of the kirsch syrup. Smooth over a quarter of the cream and press in half the cherries. Cover with a second sponge, sprinkle with more syrup, a layer of cream and the rest of the fruit. Place the third sponge on top, sprinkle with the remaining syrup and a layer of whipped cream. Cover with the last sponge layer and coat the top and sides of the whole cake with the rest of the cream. Dust the cake sides with chocolate.

Pipe the reserved cream in large rosettes on the cake surface and dot with cherries. Place a few chocolate curls in the middle to finish. Chill for 3-4 hours. Just before serving dredge a little confectioners' sugar on the chocolate curls.

BAUMKUCHEN: *This type of cake used to be baked on a rotating spit. Here it has been built up in three separate molds and cooked in wafer-thin layers under the broiler. The icing has been poured to create a roughened tree bark texture. Serve it cut in very thin slices.*

ZWETSCHKENKUCHEN: *The yeasted base of this cake also tastes delicious layered with fresh apricots. Always dredge open fruit tarts with confectioners' sugar after baking, otherwise the fruit juices soak into the pastry.*

Baumkuchen

TREE CAKE

250g/1¼ cups butter
250g/1¼ cups sugar
7 eggs, separated
2 tsp lemon zest
1 tbsp rum
50g/¼ cup ground almonds
130g/1¼ cups all-purpose flour,
    sifted
130g/⅔ cup potato flour, sifted
oil for greasing
apricot jam for brushing
lemon-flavored icing for glazing

Broiler: 350-400°F for 4-5
    mins each layer

Spit cooking was the usual method of roasting in early times, and a tree cake was quite popular. It was baked on a hand-turned, tapered, wooden spit, set in front of an open fire, and it was made of a thin batter, ladled on slowly as it cooked. Each wafer-thin layer was toasted to a golden brown color, and then another coating of fresh batter was poured on, to be toasted in its turn. The tree effect was achieved by varying the rotating speed of the spit as fresh batter was poured over. To create a rough uneven pattern, some of the cooked mixture was brushed or carved away. As many as 20-30 layers could be built up in this way, and sometimes dried and crystallized fruits were embedded in the mixture.

While the cake was still hot, thin icing was poured over it, and, once cooled, each end was trimmed straight and the wooden spit drawn out. The Baumkuchen was placed on a large elegant serving platter and a sprig of foliage inserted in the open hole at the top. Sometimes it was decorated with a great plume of finely spun sugar and the base encircled with small elegant pastries.

During the eighteenth and nineteenth centuries tree cakes reached their greatest popularity in Europe, particularly for festivals and celebrations; sometimes as many as 300 eggs were used for an especially grand occasion. Though forgotten elsewhere, Baumkuchen still remains popular in Germany today, particularly at Christmas time when Father Christmas shapes may also be found.

It has a quite special flavor and almost crispy texture because of the unique cooking method. Commercial concerns still use the old method of spit cooking with up-dated machinery, but at home we have to adapt the technique, and the modern broiler is most suitable. You can use a plain baking pan or spring-form pan for a basic cake, or you could try experimenting with different forms such as a gugelhupf or angel cake mold or with shapes that can be assembled later with apricot jam before being iced.

Beat the butter and caster sugar until pale and creamy, beat in the egg yolks one at a time, mix in the lemon zest, rum and almonds. Sift together the flours, and beat two spoonfuls at a time into the egg mixture.

Beat the egg whites in a spotlessly clean bowl until firm, then lightly fold them into the main mixture. Lightly oil the chosen cake pan (9½in diameter). Smooth 1-2 tbsp of cake batter on the base and place under the broiler. Cook until golden brown. Remove from the heat and smooth over another thin layer of mixture. Cook again. Continue toasting the layers until all the mixture is used (about 16-18 layers). Leave to cool in the pan. Unmold; brush with warm apricot jam and glaze with lemon-flavoured icing.

The cake keeps fresh for 2-3 weeks.

Zwetschkenkuchen

SWITZEN PLUM CAKE

20g/³/₄oz fresh yeast
140g/²/₃ cup milk, warmed to
    blood heat
65g/5 tbsp sugar
300g/2³/₄ cups bread flour plus
    extra for dusting
65g/5 tbsp butter
2 eggs
2 tsp grated lemon zest
pinch salt
butter for greasing and
brushing
1kg/2lb Switzen plums
25g/¹/₄ cup ground hazelnuts or
toasted bread crumbs
sugar for dredging

400°F for 35 minutes

You can use other plums and you can layer them on a sweet shortcrust pastry base; you can also scatter a streussel crumb mixture on top; and you can even serve it with whipped cream. But the genuine traditional German Zwetschkenkuchen should be made of a yeast dough base with fresh ripe Switzen plums baked in a large rectangular cake pan.

Prepare the yeast batter (p. 149). Crumble the fresh yeast into the warm milk, add a teaspoon of sugar and 75g/³/₄ cup flour taken from the main quantity. Beat well. Cover and leave to ferment for 10 minutes. Beat the butter and sugar until pale and fluffy, mix in the eggs one at a time. Then add the lemon zest. Sift the flour and salt two or three times, finally into a large bowl. Make a well in the center and put in the egg mixture, scatter over a little of the flour, then add the yeast batter. Combine well, then knead hard in the bowl or on a floured worktop until the dough starts to roll cleanly off the sides of the bowl or board and becomes very elastic and forms air bubbles. Replace in the bowl and cover with a warm cloth, or put it in a large, lightly oiled plastic bag and fasten the end. Set the dough to rise in a warm place until it has doubled in bulk.

Grease two baking pans about 8 × 12 × 1¹/₂in, and dust with flour. Divide the dough in two. Keep one half covered and roll out the other half on a floured board to fit the cake pan approximately. Line the pan with it, gently easing it into place and pushing the dough up the sides a little. Stand it uncovered in a warm place for about 20 minutes to rise again. Prepare the rest of the dough.

Prepare the fruits; wash, dry and split almost in half. Remove the stones. Lightly brush the risen pastries with melted butter and scatter over about 25g/¹/₄ cup ground hazelnuts or toasted bread crumbs. Pack in the prepared fruits close together in straight rows; they should not be opened out but left closed so that the layer of fruit is rich and juicy when it is baked. Zwetschkenkuchen tastes best while it is still slightly warm. Dredge the slices generously with sugar as you serve them.

May be frozen for up to 2 months. Defrost at room temperature for 2-3 hours.

FRANKFURTER KRANZ:
*Praline-flavored crème
pâtissière makes this plain
cake rather special.*

APFELKUCHEN: *A very
simple cake to serve for
afternoon tea.*

Streusselkuchen

CRUMB CAKE

Yeast dough (see Zwetschikenkuchen, p. 97)

Almond streussel
250g/1 cup plus 1 tbsp unsalted butter
300g/2³/₄ cups all-purpose flour, sifted
110g/1 cup ground almonds
2 tsp ground cinnamon
1 tsp lemon zest
165g/²/₃ cup sugar
confectioners' sugar for dredging

400°F for 35 minutes

Like Zwetschkenkuchen, this is a German classic. Here the yeast dough base is covered with a thick cinnamon and almond crumb covering. Streussel is made like pastry, and here are two simple ways of making it.

Prepare the yeast dough and line two baking pans as for Zwetschkenkuchen. Leave to rise.

Using a food processor Gently melt the butter and leave to cool. Drop the flour, almonds, cinnamon, lemon zest and sugar into the processor bowl and switch on for 2-3 seconds to mix well. Then quickly pour the cooled butter through the tube on to the mixture with the machine switched on. Stop the motor as soon as a crumb texture is reached.

By hand Cut the chilled butter pieces into the sifted flour and rub to fine crumbs. Use a knife to blend in the rest of the ingredients and make a coarse crumb texture. Roll into a ball, wrap and chill for 1 hour until hardened. Rub the dough through a coarse grater and dust lightly with flour to prevent it from sticking together.

Finish the cakes by brushing the risen dough with melted butter; scatter the crumb mixture generously on top. Bake in the preheated oven until well risen and golden. Cool in the pans, set on a wire rack. Dust with confectioners' sugar before serving and cut in slices.

Mohrenkopf

OTHELLO'S OR MOOR'S HEADS

4 egg yolks
50g/¹/₄ cup sugar
50g/¹/₂ cup all-purpose flour, sifted, plus extra for dusting
pinch salt
6 egg whites
50g/¹/₄ cup potato flour, sifted
150ml/²/₃ cup heavy or whipping cream
2 tbsp sugar
2 tbsp Grand Marnier or Cointreau
chocolate icing (p. 157)

400°F for 20-30 minutes

Makes 25 buns

Beat the egg yolks and half the sugar until pale and creamy. Beat in the all-purpose flour. Beat the egg whites with the salt until firm, then beat in the remaining sugar until satiny and smooth. Fold the egg snow into the first mixture, then sift over the potato flour in two stages and fold it in lightly.

Line a baking sheet with wax paper.

Fit a large pastry bag with a plain nozzle and spoon some of the mixture into it. Pipe rounds of paste about ¹/₂in across at 2in intervals. Dust with a little flour. Bake in the preheated oven until puffed and golden. Remove from the paper and cool on a wire rack. Split the cakes and scoop out a little of the pastry from the base. Beat the cream into soft peaks and whisk in the rest of the sugar and the liqueur. Place a spoonful of cream in the hollow of each split pastry and close. Prepare the soft chocolate icing (p. 157) and coat the top of each pastry with it; stand on the wire rack to set.

Desdemonas Fill with vanilla-flavored whipped cream, brush the top with strained apricot purée, and mask with kirsch-flavored white icing.

Iagos Fill the base with coffee-flavored crème pâtissière (p. 150), brush with apricot purée, and ice with coffee icing.

Chocolate beans Fill with rum-flavored chocolate cream (p. 150), cover the top with the same cream, and decorate with chocolate vermicelli.

Frankfurter Kranz

130g/9 tbsp butter
150g/²/₃ cup sugar
4 eggs, lightly beaten
2 tsp lemon zest
2 tsp rum
100g/1 cup all-purpose plain
  flour
100g/¹/₃ cup potato flour
1 tsp baking powder
2 portions vanilla buttercream
  (cooled) (p. 150) plus 50g/¹/₄
  cup unsalted butter

Praline croquant

50g/¹/₄ cup sugar
1 tbsp water
50g/¹/₂ cup flaked or chopped
  toasted almonds

6 tbsp rum, kirsch or Grand
  Marnier
glacé cherries and pistachio
  nuts for decoration

350°F for 45 minutes

This is baked in a plain ring or savarin mold.

Beat the butter and sugar until light, pale and fluffy. Beat in the egg a little at a time, beating well between each addition. Mix in the lemon zest and rum. Sift together the flours with the baking powder two or three times, then beat them into the egg mixture in three stages. The mixture should be quite firm but not stiff. Turn it into the buttered ring mold and smooth level. Bake in the preheated oven until well risen and brown and shrinking slightly from the edges of the tin. Turn out on to a wire rack to cool. Let the cake rest overnight if possible.

Prepare the buttercream (p. 150) and beat in the additional butter before combining it with the cooked buttercream.

To make the praline croquant boil the sugar and water to form a caramel (p. 151) Drop in the almonds and stir lightly to coat them with the sugar. When the mixture starts to boil, pour on to an oiled baking sheet, smooth out and leave to cool. Break the praline into pieces and chop or pound into a coarse powder.

Assemble the cake. Split the cake into four layers and brush a little alcohol on each. Reserve 3 tbsp buttercream and sandwich all the layers together with the buttercream covering the top and sides also. Sprinkle the crushed croquant all over the cake. Pipe a few rosettes on the top and decorate with cherries and pistachios.

Hobelspänne

WOOD SHAVINGS

165g/1¹/₃ cup all-purpose flour
¹/₂ tsp baking powder
40g/3 tbsp butter, cubed
25g/2 tbsp sugar
1 tsp lemon zest
1 egg
2 tbsp milk
oil for deep frying
confectioners' sugar to dredge

Makes 24 pieces

Sift together the flour and baking powder until well aerated and finally into a bowl. Drop in the butter pieces and rub to a fine crumb texture. Stir in the sugar and lemon zest. Mix in the egg and the milk and blend to a fine dough. Roll out the pastry to a thickness of ¹/₈in and cut into rectangular strips 3¹/₂ × 1in. Cut a slit about 1¹/₂in in the center of the length. Lift each pastry and carefully draw one end through the slit, gently easing it back to give a looped effect. Heat the oil to 350°F and deep fry three or four pastries at a time until golden, turning them if necessary with a perforated spoon. They take about 1¹/₂ minutes each side. Lift out the pastries and drain them on paper towels. Roll them in confectioners' sugar while they are still warm and leave to dry on a wire rack.

HOBELSPÄNNE: *This type of deep-fried pastry is very popular in Europe.*

SCHRADERPUFFER: *For a more elaborate finish, you may pour an uneven coating of rum-flavored glacé icing on this puffy ring cake.*

Bienenstich

BEESTING

130g/9 tbsp butter, melted and
    cooled
130g/¹/₂ cup plus 1 tbsp sugar
2 eggs
1 tsp lemon zest
140g/1 cup all-purpose flour
60g/¹/₃ cup (generous) potato
    flour
¹/₂ tsp baking powder

Almond toffee
50g/¹/₄ cup butter
100g/¹/₂ cup granulated sugar
125g/1 cup flaked almonds
2 tbsp milk

Vanilla cream (crème St
    Honoré)
250ml/1 cup plus 2 tbsp milk
1in vanilla pod
1 egg yolk
25g/2 tbsp cornstarch, sifted
110g/¹/₂ cup sugar
2 egg whites

325°F for 1 hour

Although Bienenstich is usually made with a yeast pastry base, the fine butter pastry in this recipe tastes just as good with a vanilla cream filling

Make the almond toffee first. Melt the butter over a low heat, then stir in the sugar and mix until it has completely dissolved. Toss in the flaked almonds and beat the mixture, adding enough milk to give a firm but spreading consistency. Leave to cool.

Prepare the vanilla cream by heating the milk with the vanilla pod, leaving it to infuse for a few minutes. Remove the pod. Beat the egg yolk with the flour and 40g/3 tbsp sugar in a heat-proof bowl, then slowly pour the hot milk over the mixture, beating all the time. Set the bowl over a pan a quarter filled with simmering water, and heat and stir the mixture until it thickens. It must not boil. Draw off the heat and pour into a bowl. Beat the egg whites until they are stiff and well peaked, beat in half the remaining sugar and fold in the rest. Lightly fold the meringue mixture into the hot cream. Cool and chill.

To make the pastry beat the cool butter and sugar until pale and fluffy; beat in the eggs one at a time blending well between each addition. Mix in the lemon zest. Sift together the flours and baking powder and blend them into the mixture 2 tbsp at a time, taking care not to over-beat. Spread the mixture on a buttered 13¹/₂ × 9¹/₂ × 1¹/₂in baking pan and smooth even. Cover with the almond toffee layer and bake in the preheated oven. Cut the cake into slices while it is still warm; leave in the pan to cool. Lift the slices out of the tin and cut each in half; sandwich together with some of the vanilla cream.

Schraderpuffer

SPONGE CUSHION

75g/¹/₃ cup butter
75g/³/₄ cup all-purpose flour,
    sifted
75g/³/₄ cup raisins
1 tsp grated lemon zest
4 eggs, separated
75g/¹/₃ cup sugar
confectioners' sugar for
    dredging

475°F for 5 minutes; then
    reduce the oven temperature
    to 425° for 10 minutes;
    finally reduce the
    temperature to 350°F for 30
    minutes

This is a speciality of Schleswig-Holstein, the most northerly point of Germany almost on the Danish border. The method of preparation and baking is quite unusual and gives a not too sweet, light and airy cake that is ideal for tea or coffee time.

Cut the butter into the flour and rub to a fine crumb texture. Toss in the raisins and lemon zest, making sure that they are well coated with flour. Set aside. Beat the egg whites in a large clean bowl until they stand in firm, snowy peaks and beat in half the sugar until the mixture is firm and glossy. Using a large metal spoon fold in the rest of the sugar and the lightly beaten egg yolks. Very carefully and lightly, fold in the flour and butter mixture in three portions. Pour the mixture into a greased and floured 8¹/₂in ring or savarin mold. Level out and bake immediately in the preheated oven. The cake puffs up high and turns a rich, golden brown. Lift out of the oven and turn out on a wire rack after 10 minutes to cool. Dust with confectioners' sugar to serve.

Käsekuchen

CURD CHEESECAKE

yeast dough (p. 149) for 2
   rectangular cake pans 8 ×
   12 × 1¹/₂in

Filling
125ml/¹/₂ cup heavy cream
50g/¹/₄ cup sugar
375g/1²/₃ cups curds cheese,
   sieved
2 eggs
pinch salt
1 tsp lemon zest
65g/¹/₂ cup raisins
25g/2 tbsp melted butter,
   cooled

400°F for 35 minutes

This traditional cake has a yeast pastry base and is baked in a rectangular pan. Because the cheese layer is thin, the flavor is much more concentrated than the familiar deep cheesecakes.

Prepare the dough and line the pans. Leave to rise a second time while you prepare the filling.
   Mix the filling by hand. Stir the cream and sugar into the cheese. Mix in the lightly beaten eggs one at a time, the salt and lemon zest, and, lastly the raisins. Divide the filling evenly between the two pans and smooth even. Trickle the butter over both surfaces and bake in the preheated oven until risen and golden. Cut in slices to serve. Will keep fresh for 2 days. Freeze while still slightly warm, wrapped in aluminum foil.

Lebkuchen

CHOCOLATE SPICED COOKIES

165g/1¹/₂ cups unblanched
   almonds, ground
50g/2oz bittersweet chocolate,
   grated
40g/¹/₃ cup candied orange and
   lemon peel, chopped small
1 tsp ground cinnamon
1 tsp ground cloves
3 egg whites
185g/1¹/₂ cups plus 1 tbsp
   confectioners' sugar, sifted
ice-cream or oblaten wafers

Icing
50g/2oz bittersweet chocolate
50g/¹/₂ cup confectioners'
   sugar, sifted

350°F for 25 minutes

Makes 60 cookies

It is customary to hang Lebkuchen on the Christmas Tree. Pierce a hole in each cookie while it is still warm.

Mix together in a bowl the almonds, chocolate, candied peels and spices. Make sure that the peels are separated and coated with nuts. Set aside.
   Beat the egg whites until they stand in firm, snowy peaks. Sift over and beat in the sugar in three stages and continue beating for about 7 minutes by machine (15 minutes by hand) until the mixture is thick, satiny and very smooth. Tip the nut mixture on to the meringue and use a large metal spoon to fold it in lightly.
   Prepare the wafers by cutting them with sharp cookie cutters into diamonds, squares or heart shapes. Pile a little of the nut meringue mixture on each of the wafers and taper it up from the sides into the middle in a dome about ¹/₂in high. Cover and leave to dry overnight in the kitchen.
   Place the cookies close together on a baking sheet — they do not rise — and bake in the preheated oven until pale golden brown.
   Meanwhile make the icing. Melt the chocolate with 1¹/₂ tbsp of water in a small bowl set over a pan of simmering water. Stir to combine. Sift the sugar into another bowl and stir in 1 tbsp hot water, then blend in the chocolate mixture and stir until smooth. Cover the bowl with a damp cloth to keep it moist. Lay the cookies to cool on a wire rack, and as soon as they are cool enough to handle, dip each one into the chocolate icing, holding it by the base.

BIENENSTICH: *This also tastes good without the pastry cream filling.*

ZIMTSTERNE, BASLER LECKERLI *and* SCHOKOLADEN-LEBKUCHEN: *Rectangular 'leckerli' and 'stars' come from Switzerland and chocolate Lebkuchen from Germany. These biscuits are typical of Christmas bakery in German-speaking regions of Europe and there are many regional specialities. In very early times, spices, dried fruits and nuts were considered to be luxury items and greatly coveted. They were imported to the West from the Orient.*

SWITZERLAND

Aargauer Rüeblitorte Basler Leckerli Zimtsterne
Bündner Kirschen Kuchen or Kirschenmichel
Truffle Torte Engadiner Nusstorte Zuger Kirschtorte
Birnbrot

Hanselmann, in St Moritz, was founded in 1894 and, together with Demels in Vienna, Sprüngli in Zürich and Rumpelmeyer in Paris, ranked as one of the finest 'café-Konditerein' in the world. Today visitors still flock to sample the delicious cakes and pastries. Here, one of the pastry cooks is adding the finishing touches to a trayful of cakes, among which there are choux buns, éclairs and japonais, as well as Mohrenkopf, vanilla slices, fruit tartlets, stuffed dates, Pretzel and doughnuts.

In the thirteenth century, the tribes fighting on the perimeters of the country we know today as Switzerland came from France, Germany and Italy. Later they were drawn together to fight a common foe — the Habsburgs — but, typical of all immigrants in a strange land, they felt the need to retain their own culture and, from the gastronomic point of view, this is still so today.

Savory *polenta, osso bucco* and spaghetti can be found in Tessin and Grisons, together with *zabaglione* and *amaretti*. The French-speaking areas have *pot au feu*, fondue, meringues and *flan aux abricots*, and the German-speaking parts have numerous dishes of German derivation, including venison in red wine sauce, semolina pudding, pear breads and *Lebkuchen*. There are, however, some specialities that the Swiss may still call their own.

In early times, much of the land was given over to a peasant agricultural economy, and the area owned by each landowner was often very large. Depending on the time of the year and the weather, whole communities would migrate. There were three types of settlement: the alpine summer village, the May-village (sometimes occupied again in the autumn) and the permanent church village. Often the school, the clergyman and the post-office moved with them leaving behind an empty village. At times their new territories extended far into neighbouring countries, which no doubt greatly influenced their cooking.

Typical of this is Grisons in the Engadine. Nestling in the south-eastern corner of Switzerland, on the borders of Italy and Austria, Grisons has a long-standing and well-founded reputation for its excellent pastry and sugar confectionary. Early Italian cooks no doubt taught and influenced the early Swiss patissiers, who in their turn passed on the knowledge to their kitchen apprentices.

While most of Switzerland remained unaffected by external disturbances, the people of Grisons suffered considerable hardship and persecution, particularly at the hands of the Habsburgs. As a result, many of the cooks emigrated, though some endeavoured to return, for there was a magical appeal about the mountains and valleys and their own Romansh language, the sole survivor of a *lingua rustica* of the Roman empire.

Switzerland celebrates more feast days than almost any other country — almost any occasion is an excuse for a festivity. Apart from the Saints' days and other holy days, there are seasonal country festivals, such as May-day, each with its appropriate savory and sweet cuisine, particularly bakery.

In Basle city center a fair is held at the end of October: almost anything from a pastry cutter for stamping out Christmas cookies to a pig, may be purchased. There

are entertainments too, and typical 'fair sweetmeats' may be bought, such as Turkish honey, sugared almonds, crocquants, rose biscuits, *Basler Leckerli*, little ball-shaped nougat and herb cakes. The peasants in the mountains have their celebrations too, for Switzerland is essentially a land of peasant stock, and many of the cakes reflect their agricultural background. Cakes are made with butter, eggs and cheese, carrots and potatoes, fruits and nuts — they are particularly fond of almonds, walnuts and chestnuts — as well as cherries, Switzen plums, apricots and apples.

The two major festivals are Christmas and carnival for the Catholic Swiss, carnival is a long and joyous occasion for the Catholic Swiss, which lasts for the three days before Lent. Young and old alike, bedecked in fancy dress and sometimes masked, parade the streets dancing, singing and merry-making. *Fasnachts chüechli* (Shrove cookies) are prepared in great quantities; they are light and crisp, sometimes spiced or flavored with almonds, deep fried or yeasted, and filled with fruit. In former times, young men would present them to their girl-friends who, in their turn, might invite the boys to a 'cake' repast. Each *Fasnacht* canton in Switzerland has its regional specialities.

Christmas, of course, saw the greatest selection of cakes. Made of nuts and mostly spiced, often perfumed with orange-flower water, rose water or kirsch, they are reminiscent of the spiced cookies of Nuremberg, for, like Austria and Germany, Switzerland was a main thoroughfare for early travellers on their long journeys from the south, over the St Gotthard Pass, to the north. It was a meeting place of a variety of cultures and also echoed the influences of the Middle East and the honey-baking traditions of the monastery kitchens.

In the late nineteenth century the Swiss discovered milk chocolate, and in 1880 chocolate in tablet form was introduced. These innovations gave the milk and cream industry a great boost, and Swiss chocolate, which eventually gained a worldwide reputation, added considerably to the bakers' repertoire. Along with the traditional cakes and biscits of the past came chocolate animals, puddings, chocolate fillings and creams for cakes; as one Swiss writer comments, 'A Swiss cookbook without chocolate recipes would be like a gugelhupf without raisins.'

Today standards of confectionery and baking in Switzerland remain high. The cakes and pastries taste as good as they always did, and the cakeshops and café-conditerei are as popular and busy as in the past. And the Swiss enthusiasm for celebrations and fairs remains; for despite their technological skills, prowess and sophistication, the Swiss remain a simple peasant nation at heart.

FASNACHT IN BASEL.
Fasching (Shrovetide) falls between the end of Epiphany and the beginning of Lent. The last three days are celebrated in the streets of the city with fancy-dress parades, wild speeches, heavy drinking and spirited fun. Special cakes are baked for the Shrovetide season; the piping revellers in this scene have Lebkuchen hearts hanging around their necks, and, in addition to various emblems of the city, their costumes are decorated with spiced honey cookie shapes. Gingerbread houses form unusual head dresses.

ZÜRICHER TIRGGELI. *These Christmas cookies are made of honey, spices, flour, sugar and rose water. The firm dough is pressed into a carved wooden baking mold before being baked.*

Bündner Kirschen Kuchen

FRESH CHERRY CAKE

*butter and 2 tsp toasted bread
    crumbs for the pan*
*3 small stale bread rolls
    (about 4 oz)*
150ml/²/₃ cup milk
*90g/7 tbsp butter, melted
    and cooled*
175g/³/₄ cup sugar
4 eggs, separated
*100g/³/₄ cup plus 1 tbsp ground
    almonds*
¹/₂ tsp ground cinnamon
*1 kg/2lb fresh, black cherries,
    washed and dried*
pinch salt
*confectioners' sugar for
    dredging*
whipped cream to serve

*350° for approximately 1-1¹/₄
    hours*

Fresh cherry cakes exist in many regions of south Germany as well as in Switzerland, but I searched a long time for this particular recipe. I ate it first when I was 17 years old and staying at a friend's house in Baden, Germany. Tante Lisbeth was a wonderful cook and excelled at baking, and for each of my frequent visits that summer she would prepare yet another special cake to tempt me. This was my favorite.

Much later, when I hoped to include the recipe in my book, Tante Lisbeth's reaction to my request was a vague wave in the direction of a regional cookery book on her shelf — 'it is there somewhere' — but she never parted with her own recipe! Last year, a friend in Switzerland came across another version of a cherry cake; it came from a hand-written manuscript of the late nineteenth century. Here at last was the very cake I so fondly remembered; it tastes every bit as good now as it did all those years ago.

Prepare a 9¹/₂in spring-form pan. Butter well and coat with 2 tbsp toasted bread crumbs. Break the bread rolls into pieces and place them in a bowl. Heat the milk with 140ml/²/₃ cup water and pour the liquid on to the rolls. Leave to soak for about 15 minutes. Pour the melted butter into a mixing bowl, leaving the sediment behind, mix in the sugar and egg yolks and beat until the mixture is pale and creamy. Beat in the almonds and cinnamon. Drain the bread rolls, squeezing out any excess moisture by hand. Break them up small with a fork or blend in a food proccessor bowl for a few seconds. Beat the paste into the main mixture. Stir in the cherries. Beat the egg whites with the salt in a clean bowl until they hold firm, snowy peaks. Using a large metal spoon, lightly fold the egg snow into the cherry batter. Pour the batter into the prepared cake pan. Bake until golden.

The cake may be eaten warm or cold. Dredge with confectioners' sugar and serve with whipped cream on the side. It also freezes very well for up to 2 months.

Zuger Kirschtorte

Nut meringue layer
4 egg whites
130g/1 cup plus 1 tbsp
confectioners' sugar, sifted
150g/1 cup unblanched
almonds, freshly ground
1 tbsp all-purpose flour
1 tbsp potato flour
1 tsp heaped cocoa powder

350° for 15 minutes

Sponge layer
4 eggs, separated
110g/$\frac{1}{2}$ cup sugar
65g/$\frac{1}{2}$ cup all-purpose plain
flour
65g/$\frac{1}{3}$ cup potato flour
75g/$\frac{1}{3}$ cup unsalted butter,
melted and cooled

350° for 45 minutes

1 portion basic buttercream
(p. 150)
2 tbsp toasted almond flakes
confectioners' sugar for dredging

1 tbsp redcurrent or raspberry
jam
4 tbsp kirsch

Syrup
3 tbsp sugar
6 tbsp water
6-8 tbsp kirsch

This luxurious Torte is laced with kirsch.

Prepare the nut meringue layers (p. 140). Sift the cocoa powder in with the flours and ground almonds before folding them into the beaten egg whites. Divide the mixture equally, and bake two 8$\frac{1}{2}$in flat discs on wax paper until golden. Remove from the papers and leave to cool on wire racks.

Prepare the sponge layer (p. 145). Grease and line a 8$\frac{1}{2}$in spring-form pan with wax paper. Grease the paper, pour in the mixture and bake. Cool on a wire rack.

Make the basic buttercream (p. 150). Blend in the jam and kirsch. Chill for a short time, but it should still be workable.

Make the syrup (p. 151) by dissolving 3 tbsp sugar in 6 tbsp water and cook to the thread stage (215°F). Cool and stir in 6-8 tbsp kirsch.

To assemble the cake trim the sponge cake flat and even if necessary, and sprinkle with half the syrup. Spread about a quarter of the buttercream over one nut meringue and turn the sponge layer, syrup side down, on to it. Sprinkle the rest of the syrup over the sponge

and smooth over a further layer of buttercream. Cover with the second meringue. Spread the remainder of the buttercream over the top and sides of the cake. Press 2 tbsp toasted almond flakes around the sides of the cake. Dredge a heavy coating of confectioners' sugar on the cake top and, using the back of a long-bladed knife, emboss the traditional diamond trellis pattern in the cream surface. Leave the cake to mature for at least a day before cutting. It keeps well for up to a week.

AARGAUER RÜEBLITORTE:
*This is a delicious
carrot-cake. In past
centuries, root vegetables
were almost as common as
fruit in sweet dishes. Ask
your friends to guess what
the mystery ingredient is in
this cake — they will be
quite surprised.*

Basler Leckerli

*165g/1⅓ cup all-purpose flour,
    sifted, plus extra for dusting*
½ tsp baking soda
100g/⅓ cup mature dark honey
100g/⅓ cup plus 1 tbsp sugar
1 tsp ground cinnamon
pinch cloves
pinch nutmeg
*50g/½ cup flaked or nibbed
    almonds*
*25g/1½ tbsp candied orange
    and lemon peel, chopped
    small*
*1 tsp coarsely chopped
    lemon zest*
50ml/¼ cup kirsch
3 tbsp sugar for syrup

400°F for 15 minutes

Makes 28 pieces

Basler Leckerli originated, it seems, in the mid-fifteenth century when 300 church noblemen gathered for the Council of Basel in an attempt to overthrow the Pope's absolute supremacy. The local guild of Lebkuchen manufacturers considered that their familiar spiced Lebkuchen were too mundane for the illustrious guests of the city, and they decided to invent a new 'Leckerl', mouth-watering cookie. They added candied orange and lemon peels and almonds to the basic mixture.

In later times it became customary to prepare the various Christmas cookies at home. It was a pre-Christmas occupation for the whole family as all the ingredients had to be prepared by hand — how many hours it must have taken to peel the almonds and cut them into slivers. The quantities, too, were considerable, and beating the mixtures without the aid of modern machinery was laborious work. A local writer mentions that her grandmother used to employ the porter from the local railway station to take on the heavy task. Today, although the tradition lingers, Leckerli are manufactured commercially and are a Christmas delicacy throughout the world.

Sift together the flour and baking soda. Set aside. Gently heat the honey, sugar and spices in a large pan until the sugar has dissolved. Bring to almost boiling. Lower the heat and stir in the almonds, candied orange and lemon peels and chopped lemon zest. Remove from the heat and beat in 100g/¾ cup of the flour mixture. Sift the remaining flour on to a work-surface, make a well in the middle and pour in the warm mixture. Quickly blend it all together. Roll out the dough to ½in thick and line a flour-dusted 7 × 11in baking tray. Leave to rest and mature overnight. Bake in the preheated oven.

Using a sharp knife, cut into the hot pastry about three-quarters of their depth into 1½ squares. Lift the pastry from the tray on to a wire rack.

Make a syrup, boiled to the thread stage (p. 151), with 40g/3 tbsp sugar and 25ml/2 tbsp water. Cut through the pastry edges and brush on the pastries with syrup while still hot. Leave to cool.

These will keep for several weeks stored in an air-tight container.

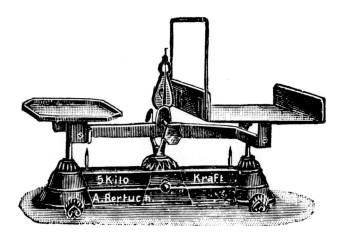

Aargauer Rüeblitorte

CARROT CAKE

6 egg yolks
75g/³⁄₄ cup confectioners'
    sugar, sifted, plus extra for
    dredging
1 tsp lemon zest
pinch salt
200g/7oz carrots, peeled
110g/1 cup roasted hazelnuts,
    ground
110g/1 cup ground almonds
25g/2 tbsp potato flour
1 tsp baking powder
1 tsp ground cinnamon
pinch ground cloves
2 tbsp kirsch
4 egg whites
75g/¹⁄₃ cup sugar
whipped cream to serve

350°F for 1 hour

Beat the egg yolks with the confectioners' sugar, lemon zest and salt until pale and creamy. Grate the carrots, drain any liquid and pat dry with paper towels. Stir into the egg and sugar with the hazelnuts and almonds. Sift the flour with the baking powder and spices and blend with the mixture. Mix in the kirsch.

Beat the egg whites until softly peaked; sift in the sugar and beat until the mixture looks satiny and smooth. Fold the meringue into the carrot mixture lightly and carefully. Pour into a greased and floured 9½in spring-form pan and bake. Cool on a wire rack. Dredge with more sugar before serving. Do not cut the cake for at least 3 days, so that the flavors may mature. Offer whipped cream on the side.

In Switzerland it is the custom to finish the cake with a white glacé or fondant icing and to decorate it with marzipan carrots.

Brush the warm cake with strained apricot jam and coat with fondant icing (p. 154). Tint a little marzipan with orange food coloring and make 13 small carrot shapes. Use angelica for the stems. Lay the carrots on the icing before it has set; one for each slice of cake is fun. Lay three in the middle of the cake and the other ten around the outside.

Zimtsterne

CINNAMON STARS

2 egg whites
250g/1 cup plus 2 tbsp sugar
250g/2 cups unblanched
    almonds, coarsely ground
1 tbsp ground cinnamon
1½ tbsp kirsch

400°F for 15 minutes

Makes 30 cookies

Another Christmas speciality.

Beat the egg whites until stiff, then mix in the sugar and beat for about 10 minutes by machine (20 minutes by hand) until the mixture is very thick, white and highly glossed. Reserve about 6 tbsp of the mixture. Mix the almonds, spice and kirsch into the rest of the snow. Gather into a ball, cover and chill for 30 minutes. Roll the paste out on a sugared board to ³⁄₈in thick, and cut out star shapes with a cookie cutter. Transfer the cookies to a lightly buttered, wax paper baking sheet and smooth some of the reserved meringue on top of each. Bake. Cool on a wire rack. These cookies keep for several weeks stored in an air-tight container.

Zimtsterne are often used as Christmas tree decorations. Use a cocktail stick or skewer to pierce a hole in the top of each cookie before baking.

ZUGER KIRSCHTORTE:
Always be generous with the kirsch in this recipe, for without a strong cherry 'kick' it is inclined to taste bland.

BÜNDNER KIRSCHEN KUCHEN: *A lovely moist cherry cake, to be served with lashings of whipped cream.*

BIRNBROT: *Dried pears, prunes, dates and figs are more common in continental fruit breads. In this loaf yeast dough binds the fruits together.*

Engadiner Nusstorte

*sweet shortcrust pastry (p. 145)
for a 9¹/₂in spring-form pan*

Filling
*250g/1 cup plus 2 tbsp sugar
225g/2 cups walnuts, coarsely
chopped
300ml/2³/₄ cups heavy cream
1 tbsp honey
50g/ ¹/₃ cup candied orange and
lemon peel, chopped
1 lightly beaten egg white*

350° for 1 hour

Almost every Swiss cookery book includes a version of this deceptively simple walnut tart. Sandwiched between layers of short-crust pastry, is a most delicious filling made of honey, walnuts and cream. The cake originates in the Engadin, a region famous for its pastry chefs, and it is still popular today.

Make the pastry and chill it while you prepare the filling. Cook the sugar in a large, heavy-based skillet over low heat, and stir until it turns to a pale golden caramel. Drop in the walnuts, stir and coat them well with the syrup for 2-3 minutes. Pour on the cream. Combine well and mix in the honey and candied fruits. Set aside to cool.

Roll out two-thirds of the pastry and line the base and 2in up the sides of the greased cake pan (see above); brush with the egg white. Spread the cooled filling evenly over the base and lift up and fold the surplus edge of pastry over the top of the filling all round the edges. Brush with water. Roll out the rest of the pastry to cover the walnut filling and lay it on top of the filling, making sure that the sides stick well. Prick the pastry lid all over with a fork, which is traditional. Bake until just colored; if necessary, cover with foil towards the end of the cooking time. Allow to mature for 3-4 days before cutting. Keeps well for at least 1 month.

Truffle Torte

CHOCOLATE TRUFFLE CAKE

*165g/5¹/₂oz dark bittersweet
chocolate, melted and
cooled
2 tsp instant coffee
100g/7 tbsp butter, softened
130g/¹/₂ cup plus 1 tbsp sugar
4 eggs, separated
100g/³/₄ cup toasted hazelnuts,
ground
1¹/₂ portions whipped chocolate
cream flavored with coffee
liqueur (p. 150)
cocoa powder for dredging
mimosa balls or whole
caramelized hazelnuts to
decorate*

325° for 1 hour 15 minutes

Break the chocolate into pieces and place them in a small heat-proof bowl with the instant coffee and 6 tbsp boiling water. Set the bowl over a pan of simmering water to melt the chocolate. Stir gently to blend, then set aside to cool.

Mix the butter and sugar until pale and creamy. Beat in the egg yolks one at a time and continue beating until the mixture is very thick and pale in color. Beat in the cool chocolate liquid and hazelnuts. Beat the egg whites separately until they are stiff, and fold them lightly and carefully into the chocolate mixture. Butter and line an 8¹/₂in spring-form pan with wax paper. Butter the paper and pour in the mixture and bake immediately. Wait 10 minutes before turning out to cool.

The cake should feel quite moist. When cold, wrap in plastic wrap and chill for 2 days.

Assemble the cake a day before it is needed.

Make the whipped chocolate cream. Split the cake into three layers. Reserve about one-third of the cream for the top and sides of the cake and use the rest to sandwich the three layers. Fit a pastry bag with a large plain nozzle and spoon about 5 tbsp cream into the bag. Smooth the rest of the cream on the sides and top of the cake. Pipe five thick, straight and parallel lines across the top of the cake and dredge generously all over with cocoa powder. Stud the mimosa balls or hazelnuts along the piped lines. Cover and chill overnight before serving.

Birnbrot

CHRISTMAS PEAR AND NUT BREAD

250g/9oz dried pears
110g/4oz dried prunes
110g/4oz dried figs, chopped
　small
110g/4oz dried or fresh dates,
　without stones
75g/¹/₂ cup chopped candied
　orange and lemon peel,
　chopped
110g/²/₃ cup raisins
110g/²/₃ cup golden raisins
1 tbsp pine nuts
75g/²/₃ cup hazelnuts, toasted
　and chopped coarsely
75g/²/₃ cup walnuts, chopped
　coarsely
1 tsp lemon zest
2 tsp orange zest
25ml/2 tbsp kirsch or rum

Bread dough
20g/³/₄oz fresh yeast
250g/1³/₄ cups bread flour plus
　extra for dusting
60g/5 tbsp sugar
pinch salt
1¹/₂ tsp cinnamon
large pinch clove
¹/₂ tsp ground star aniseed or
　allspice
2in vanilla pod, split

2 tbsp sugar
1 tbsp cornstarch
2 tbsp kirsch or rum

350° for 1 hour

This fruit bread of peasant origins is very popular throughout Switzerland for Christmas. Known as Birnenweggen, Dörrbirnenfladen and Früchtebrot, it is also found in south Germany and Austria as Hutzelbrot and Kletzenbrot. The main ingredient is dried pears, with prunes, dates, figs, golden raisins and raisins, candied peels, nuts and spices making up the rest. The rich fruit mixture is held together by a plain yeasted bread dough, and it is baked in loaf form or as small buns. Large quantities are prepared, enough to last until Candlemas at the beginning of February.

The bread bears some resemblance to a British Candlemas cake, but the regional preferences are particularly evident. In America and Britain a creamed butter, sugar and egg mixture, rather than dough, binds the fruits together. The large dried fruits, spices and nuts are left out, and while we like brandy or rum, they prefer eau de vie of kirsch or pears.

Dried pears may be bought in health-food shops and delicatessen stores.

Bake the Birnbrot 3-4 weeks before Christmas. Wrap closely in foil and store in a cool place.

Carefully wash the pears and prunes. Place them in a pan and just cover with water. Leave to soften for 2-3 hours. Set the pan on the heat, bring to the boil and simmer gently for about 20 minutes. Drain the fruits but reserve the juice and leave to cool. Chop up the figs.

Place the figs, dates, orange and lemon peels, raisins, golden raisins, the pine nuts, hazelnuts, walnuts, lemon and orange zests in a large bowl. Toss well together to mix and pour on the kirsch or rum. Chop up the cooled fruit roughly and remove the stones. Add to the fruit and nut mixture.

Make a sponge batter (p. 149) with 50ml/2fl oz of the reserved fruit syrup, warmed to blood heat, yeast, 50g/¹/₂ cup flour and 1 tsp sugar taken from the main quantity. Cover and set aside to rise and double in bulk. Meanwhile, sift the remaining flour with the salt and spices in a large bowl. Make a well in the center, pour in the sponge batter and draw in a little of the flour. Scoop in the seeds of the split vanilla pod and sugar. Combine well together and moisten with about 100ml/1/³ cup of the fruit syrup. Knead the dough very thoroughly until it becomes less sticky and starts to roll off the sides of the bowl. When it is very elastic and large air-bubbles have started to form, gather into a large ball and place on the flour-dusted work-top.

Pull the dough out and gradually knead in the fruit and nut mixture until all has been used. Roll into a large ball and lay in the large flour-dusted bowl. Dredge with a little more flour and cover with a clean dish cloth. Set aside in a cool place to rise overnight.

Next day, break off pieces of dough and form into hand-sized 1¹/₂-2in rolls, or make two larger loaves (for 8¹/₂ × 4¹/₂ × 2¹/₂ loaf pans), according to your choice. Lay small rolls, well apart, on greased baking sheets. Leave to rest and rise a little for 15-20 minutes, then bake in the pre heated oven until golden and well risen.

Kirsch glaze for the warm loaves. Heat 250ml/1 cup fruit syrup with 2 tbsp sugar, bring to the boil. Stir in 1 tbsp cornstarch and cook until thickened. Draw off the heat and stir in 2 tbsp kirsch. Brush on the warm loaves, press in a few almond halves for decoration, and leave to cool.

Serve cut in thin slices with coffee or tea or even a glass of red wine. It also tastes good spread with butter.

THANKSGIVING GREETINGS.

AMERICA

Blueberry Tart Raisin Chocolate Fudge Cake Sunshine Cake
Pumpkin Pie Butterscotch Pie
Chilled Sultana and Orange Cheesecake
Strawberry Shortcake Eliza Leslie's Ginger Cup Cakes
Fastnachts

The Amish people first came to Pennysylvania, in New England, in the seventeenth century. They had left Rhineland Germany, Switzerland, and the Austro-Hungarian empire as a result of religious persecution. In the New World they retained their cultural and religious beliefs and followed a simple life. Like the British Pilgrim Fathers, the Amish had austere religious precepts, but they were very interested in cooking and eating, and food became almost a religious symbol. The settlers learned about the local produce from the American Indians and pumpkins grew there in abundance. The Pennsylvania Dutch pumpkin pie is now an American classic and together with turkey has become part of the traditional Thanksgiving repast.

Modern American cooking and baking is an amalgam of all the cultures that met together in the New World from the early seventeenth century onwards. Before that time the native Indians had made the most of the rich produce the land offered. Indian corn and maple syrup were their important staples, but they also used roots, parsley, leeks, wild berries and rice, pumpkins, nasturtium and marigold flowers, and wild liquorice, mulberries, rose hips and peanuts. But two particular groups must be credited with establishing American gastronomy in those early colonial times. First came the British pilgrims, seeking religious freedom, who settled in New England in 1620. Then the Mennonites or Old Order Amish from Rhineland Germany, Switzerland, Moravia and other parts of the Austro-Hungarian territories, established Germantown in Pennsylvania.

Both communities were anxious to retain their traditional ways of life. However, they accepted the need to use local produce and were grateful to be instructed by the native Indians in their customs and ways of preparing foods with unfamiliar ingredients. Many of the British pilgrims came from urban backgrounds, and the women had to learn new skills, to raise poultry and care for dairy animals as well as how to butcher them. Local fish — sturgeon, oyster, shrimp and lobster — and varieties of fowl were plentiful, and there was good butter, cheese and vegetables, as well as the local produce. They had brought seeds from England and planted the familiar cabbages, turnips, onions, parsnips, peas, carrots, herbs and even beans.

Inspiration for much of their home cooking came from the English cookery books that they had carried across the ocean, and although the more affluent had brought their beloved spices (cinnamon, ginger, mace, clove and pepper), savory and sweet foods alike were essentially rather plain and unimaginative, if of good quality, and typical of seventeenth and eighteenth century fare in England. Gradually a distinctive New World influence emerged as the pilgrims grew wild grapes and strawberries, melons, squash, different colored corns — white, blue and yellow — tomatoes and sweet potatoes. Early corn recipes of Indian origin produced primitive ash or hoe cakes, baked on a hoe in front of the fire, cornstick, Johnny cake and deep-fried hushpuppies. Corn puddings, made with eggs, milk, honey or maple syrup and nutmeg, became a uniquely American way to end a meal. Later, corn was used with flour, lard and water to make a kind of dough crust to cover a 'pandowdy'. This typical apple pudding, flavored with maple syrup, diced pork and nutmeg and topped with thick cream and a shaving of maple sugar, would be served along with baked beans at breakfast.

British-style meat pies were also baked in the pre heated brick ovens; and a century later a writer noted a New England housewife's mortification if a visitor 'caught them without pie in the house'. It is agreed, however, that pies were also introduced by the other group of immigrants, the Pennsylvania Dutch or Plain People as the early settlers were known. (Later refugees were nicknamed the 'fancy' or 'gay' Dutch.) Their religious ways may have been austere, but their lifestyle was the very opposite. Wherever they travelled and settled throughout America they influenced local cuisine, enriching both the plain colonial dishes of the English and those borrowed from the Indians too; and as enthusiastic as they were to offer new inspiration, they were also eager to assimilate and make the most of what was unfamiliar and strange to them.

Most credit must go to the Pennsylvania Dutch for their introduction of 'dessert' fare to the American table. In Germanic Europe no meal, not even among the poorest people, ended without dessert and even the early settlers in the New World insisted on including something sweet. They brought spices from Europe — cinnamon being the most coveted — and cinnamon buns, gingerbread, snaps and cake, sweet rolls and doughnuts were common fare in the early kitchens and were served at all kinds of meals and celebrations. They learned to combine the spices with the new nuts and fruits; black walnuts, for example. And pies became great favourites. Today as many as fifty different pies are credited to Dutch cooks; among them are cranberry, huckleberry and green currant, butterscotch, custard, pumpkin, rhubarb, berry and shoo-fly (molasses).

In the nineteenth century yet another pioneer had great influence — Johnny Appleseed. He planted apple trees in Indiana and more than anyone else helped to turn America into apple country. Here was more wonderful 'pie timber' (the popular expression given to a pie filling at the time), which eventually became the most popular American dessert; apple pie. To quote a cookery book of southern cooking in the early 1900s:

> Ask the average man what he prefers for dessert, and almost invariably he will answer 'pie'. In an hotel or restaurant, when he looks over the menu he usually chooses 'pie'. If there is an apple pie he usually goes no further but stops there — and 'pie' it is.

As the saying goes, 'seven sweets and seven sours' constituted a 'Dutch' meal. The Pennsylvania Dutch loved to eat well and to great excess. In early times at least a dozen dishes would be set out on the table (there were three meals a day) before the diners sat down, and there was nothing strange about eating sausage with a slice of apple pie, much as the English eat cheese. There was an abundance of good food and no end to good eating at this time.

This imaginary description of the sweet courses in a Pennsylvania Dutch meal appears in Washington Irving's *Legend of Sleepy Hollow*, published in 1820.

> To his devouring mind's eye he pictured . . . the ample charms of a genuine Dutch country tea-table in the sumptuous time of autumn. Such heaped up platters of cakes of various and almost indescribable kinds, known only to experienced Dutch housewives! There was the doughty dough-nut, the tender olyloek, and the crisp and crumbling cruller; sweet-cakes and short-cakes, ginger-cakes and honey-cakes, and the whole family of cakes. And then there were apple pies and peach pies and pumpkin pies, besides slices of ham and smoked beef; and moreover delectable dishes of preserved plums and peaches and pears and quinces; not to mention broiled shad and roasted chickens; together with bowls of milk and cream, all mingled higgledy-piggledy, pretty much as I have enumerated them, with the motherly tea-pot sending up its clouds of vapor from the midst.

'Cake sales' became part of everyday life in the local communities. School events, church functions, agricultural and state fairs — each occasion offered an opportunity to the housewife to show off her skill and outdo her neighbour with a variety of cakes that reflected all the influences of their different cultures. They were all fine cooks and bakers, and the competition was fierce but rewarding for those serious eaters.

The liking for all things sweet had begun to grow at the end of the eighteenth century, and maple sugar became a luxury product. As recipes in cookery books showed more and more sugar being used, so the number of recipes for desserts increased substantially.

'Lighter' cakes, invented locally, appeared with the discovery in the 1850s of chemical leavening agents, cream of tartar and baking powder, which made a cake lighter, for it rose much higher, and reduced preparation and baking time. But it was simply a 'puffy debasement', as Karen Hess suggests, of the lovely rich, yeasted egg-light and nutty cake mixtures of the 'Dutch' past.

The 1870s saw another doubtful introduction to American desserts from Mrs J.H. Kellog. Endeavouring to combat the 'dietetic evils of pastries', she invented a 'cereal pie crust' using her husband's products. So successful was her campaign that today only a few American pie crusts are still made of butter and lard.

The beginning of the twentieth century saw a fresh influx of immigrants to America, bringing with them new culinary inspirations to add to the already rich assortment. Austrians and Hungarians, arriving from the crumbling Empire, brought their own sumptuous confections, and Scandinavian cooks brought their simpler, flaky and buttery coffee breads and cakes, coffee rings and buns oozing with sugar and filled with nuts and dried fruits. 'Danish' was to become as ubiquitous to the coffee break and *Kaffeeklatsch* as apple pie to dessert.

Today dessert is as popular as ever in America; despite the many convenience and fast-food usurpers, enough of the native American and improved European traditions remain to remind us of the rich heritage of American home baking.

A large cup of steaming hot coffee at the breakfast bar.

Raisin Chocolate Fudge Cake

65g/5 tbsp butter

200g/³/₄ cup plus 2 tbsp brown sugar

1 whole egg

2 tbsp orange juice, sieved

2 tsp orange zest

50g/2oz chocolate, melted and cooled

60ml/¹/₄ cup milk

pinch baking soda

140g/1 cup plus 1 tbsp all-purpose flour, sifted

¹/₂ tsp baking powder

¹/₂ tsp ground cinnamon

¹/₄ tsp ground cloves

75g/²/₃ cup raisins

50g/¹/₂ cup flaked almonds

Filling

1 portion cooled buttercream with yolks (p. 150)

75g/³/₄ cup pecan nuts, chopped

50g/²/₃ cup grated coconut

75g/²/₃ cup raisins, cut in half

pecan halves and flaked almonds to decorate

350° for 1 hour

Cream the butter and half the sugar. Beat in the egg, blend well. Add the orange juice and zest. Beat in the rest of the sugar and the chocolate. Combine well. Mix the milk with ¹/₄ cup water and blend in the baking soda. Sieve together the flour and baking powder with the cinnamon and cloves. Dust the almonds and raisins with some of the flour and set aside. Beat one-third of the liquid into the mixture followed by one-third of the dry ingredients. Repeat in two further stages. Mix in the raisins and almonds. Turn into a 3in deep layer pan, ready-greased and fully wax paper-lined 8¹/₂in in diameter. Level the surface. Bake in the preheated oven until risen and shrinking away slightly from the edges of the tin. Cool on a wire rack.

Make the filling. Into the cooled cream (p. 150) mix the pecan nuts, coconut and raisins.

To assemble, split the cake into three layers. Reserve just over one-third of the filling for the outside and use the remainder to sandwich the three chocolate layers together. Smooth the rest on the top and sides of the cake. Decorate with pecans and almond flakes.

The cake should settle for at least a day before it is cut. It will stay fresh for up to a week.

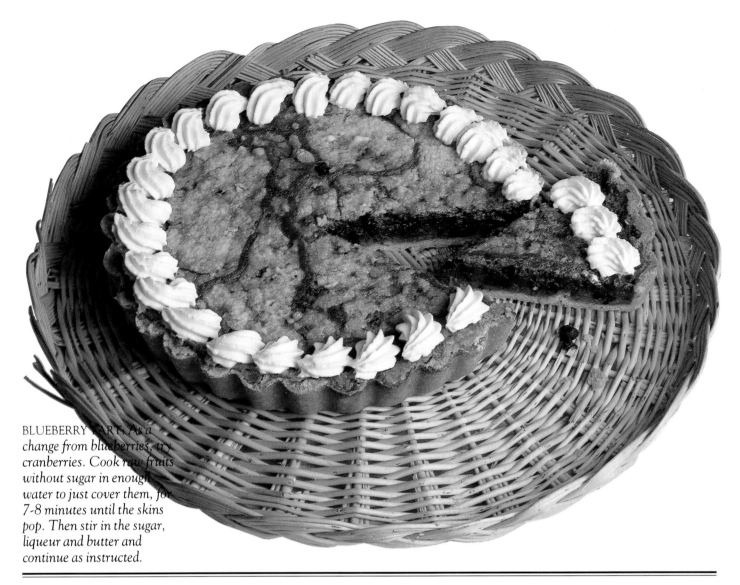

BLUEBERRY TART. As a change from blueberries, try cranberries. Cook raw fruits without sugar in enough water to just cover them, for 7-8 minutes until the skins pop. Then stir in the sugar, liqueur and butter and continue as instructed.

Blueberry Tart

sweet shortcrust pastry for a
    8½in tart pan (p. 145)
50g/½ cup ground almonds
50g/½ cup confectioners' sugar

Filling
400g/14oz blueberries, fresh
    or frozen
140g/⅔ cup sugar
2 tbsp Grand Marnier or
    Cointreau
110g/½ cup butter
3 eggs
2 tbsp cornstarch or potato
    flour, sifted
65ml/5 tbsp heavy cream
2 tsp orange zest
2 tbsp lemon juice
sweetened whipped cream to
    serve

350° for 1 hour

Defrost the fruit, if necessary, and drain off the surplus juice. Line the base and 1in up the sides of a greased tart pan with shortcrust pastry. Prick all over with a fork. Chill.

Make the filling. Drop the blueberries, 3 tbsp sugar, liqueur and 3 tbsp butter into a pan, heat and stir gently until the fruit has slightly caramelized. Leave to cool. Beat together the remaining butter and sugar until pale and fluffy; beat in the eggs one at a time, add the flour and cream. Mix in the orange zest and lemon juice, then fold in the blueberry mixture. Scatter the ground almonds over the base of the pastry shell and pour in the prepared filling. Dredge with the confectioners' sugar and bake in the pre-heated oven. Leave to cook in the pan.

Serve with sweetened whipped cream on the side.

Eliza Leslie's Ginger Cup Cakes

110g/¹/₂ cup butter
100g/¹/₃ cup light brown sugar
175ml/¹/₂ cup molasses
200g/1³/₄ cups all-purpose flour
1 tsp baking soda
¹/₂ tsp ground allspice
1 tsp ground cloves
2 tsp ground ginger
1 egg
1 egg yolk
4 tbsp milk

325° for 30 minutes

Makes 28 cup cakes

This is a modern interpretation of a recipe in Eliza Leslie's *Seventy-Five Receipts for Pastry, cakes and sweetmeats by a lady of Philadelphia*, published in 1828. It emphasizes the fast-growing predeliction for much sweeter cakes in America. I have halved the quantity of powdered spices.

Gently heat the butter, sugar and molasses in a pan until the butter has melted and the sugar dissolved. (Do not boil or the cakes will be hard.) Draw off the heat to cool. Sift together two or three times, the flour, soda, allspice, cloves and ginger, finally into a large bowl. Make a well in the middle.

Beat the egg and egg yolk with about half the milk and pour the mixture into the flour with the cooled syrup. Beat to a smooth batter, adding more milk if necessary.

Use paper baking cups and fill each no more than half full with the mixture, which rises a lot during baking. Bake until well risen. The cakes should feel slightly soft to the touch. Leave to cool on wire racks.

Sunshine Cake

165g/5¹/₂oz plain flour, sifted, plus extra for the pan
pinch salt
6 eggs, separated
2in vanilla pod
1 tsp cream of tartar
250g/1 cup plus 2 tbsp sugar
1 tsp lemon juice, strained
confectioners' sugar to serve

350° for 50 minutes

Sunshine cake reminds me of my childhood. I attended dancing classes for many years and at the end of each summer term we performed a display for our parents. One year we tap-danced to an American ditty, '. . . we ought to bake a sunshine cake, it isn't really so hard to make . . .'

Carefully wash and dry a 9in angel food cake pan and dust with flour.

Sift the flour and salt several times to aerate well. Beat the egg yolks until thick and frothy, then mix in the seeds of the vanilla pod. Set aside. Lightly beat the egg whites in a spotlessly clean bowl until they are foamy, add the cream of tartar and continue whisking until they have expanded into firm white peaks. Sift 75g/¹/₃ cup of sugar over the egg whites and beat in until glossy and smooth. Continue by hand.

Using a large metal spoon, carefully fold in the beaten egg yolks and lemon juice. Sift over one-third of the flour and gently fold it in; repeat in two more stages.

Pour the sponge batter into the floured mold. Drag a knife through it to break any pockets of air. Bake. When well risen and springy to the touch, turn over to balance on a small inverted funnel or a wire rack to cool, leaving the cake pan in place.

Dredge with confectioners' sugar to serve.

Pumpkin Pie

350ml/1¹/₂ cups pumpkin purée
(see below)
3 eggs lightly beaten
100g/7 tbsp sugar
500ml/2¹/₄ heavy cream
¹/₂ tsp ground mace
¹/₂ tsp ground nutmeg
1 tsp ground ginger
2 tbsp sherry or rum
1 par-baked tart case of sweet,
shortcrust pastry in a 8¹/₂in
pan (p. 145); make enough
pastry for a 9¹/₂-10¹/₂in tart
pan and reserve one-third of
the pastry
1 lightly beaten egg white for
brushing

375° for 25 minutes

Many seventeenth and eighteenth century recipe books were taken to America from England by the colonists, and Eliza Smith's *The Compleat Housewife* was the first English book to be republished in an American edition in 1742. It was not until 1796 that *American Cookery* was published, followed later in the same year by a second, enlarged and much improved edition. The authoress, Amelia Simmons, a native of America, had gathered together, initially, a modest collection of 130 recipes, and although many had been borrowed from English cookery books, there was also a selection of original American recipes not seen in print before.

Here we find a tart made of 'cramberries' as well as 'cramberry' sauce offered with turkey. Indian slapjacks, 'johnny' cake and Indian pudding are all made with Indian oatmeal, an American staple rarely used in England. She also gives the recipe for a splendid Independence cake, decorated with gold leaf, full of eggs, dried fruits, spices, brandy and wine, and raised with yeast. Her gingerbread recipe, though obviously not original, was the first to use an artificial raising agent, pearl-ash.

Included in the pudding section were two recipes for that 'great American dessert' — 'pompkin' [pie]. The first recipe was for more elaborate occasions as it included sugar, an expensive commodity in those days, and cream. The second used the commonly available molasses and milk.

Pumpkin pie is now served as a traditional Thanksgiving Day dessert.

To prepare the pumpkin purée, peel, slice and remove the seeds from a pumpkin. Cut into cubes and boil in lightly salted water until soft. Drain well. Push through a fine sieve.

Leave to cool. Beat together the purée, eggs and sugar until well blended. Mix in the cream, mace, nutmeg, ginger and sherry or rum and combine well. Pour into the prepared flan case.

Roll out the reserved pastry to ¹/₄in and cut two long strips 1in wide for the edge. Cut the rest with a fluted pastry wheel into ¹/₂in strips and lay in trellis fashion on the pie. Cover the edges with the plain pastry strips. Brush with lightly beaten egg white and bake until it has just set. Serve warm.

SUNSHINE CAKE (T) RAISIN CHOCOLATE FUDGE CAKE (R) GINGER CUP CAKES (L): *Sunshine cake may be served with fresh berries, or stewed fruits and cream. The other cakes in this picture are typical old American recipes combining traditional ingredients brought by immigrants from Europe with native American specialities.*

Fastnachts

DOUGHNUTS

250ml/1 cup plus 2 tbsp milk,
    warmed to blood heat, plus
    extra for brushing
25g/1oz fresh yeast
400g/3½ cups bread flour,
    sifted, plus extra for dusting
2 tbsp sugar
8 egg yolks, lightly beaten
100g/7 tbsp butter
½ tsp salt
1 tbsp brandy
1 tsp rose water
rose conserve or raspberry jam
    for the filling
vegetable oil for deep frying
sugar for dredging

Makes 28 doughnuts

The Rhinelanders of Germany began emigrating to Pennsylvania in the seventeenth century when the religious persecutions and deprivation in their native land had become intolerable. In the years that followed, and as more people came to the New World, the community started to rebuild its life and reassert its ethnic culture and traditions.

The Pennsylvania Dutch, as they were known, brought *Fastnachts* with them from the Old World, delicious yeasted doughnuts, which were baked for Shrovetide and Christmas. Doughnuts originated in Europe during the seventeenth century, and they were baked at first only for the major festivals, particularly Christmas and Shrovetide, or *Fasching*, as it was known in Teutonic Europe.

Here is an original recipe that uses yeast. I urge you to try a Pennsylvania Dutch *Fastnacht* — it is worth the effort. All the ingredients should be at room temperature before baking commences and the flour warmed (p. 149).

Prepare a yeast batter (p. 149) with 75ml/⅓ cup milk, the yeast, 100g/⅓ cup flour and 1 tsp of sugar. Beat well. Set aside to ferment. Mix half the remaining milk with the egg yolks and set aside. Melt the butter in the rest of the milk. Cool to lukewarm.

Sift together the rest of the flour with the salt into a large bowl and make a well in the center. Stir in the rest of the sugar, the fermented yeast and the milk mixture. Blend all together and beat well until the dough thickens. Add the brandy and rose water and continue beating until the dough texture is smooth, shiny and will drop off a spoon. Take out half the mixture and cover the bowl with a warm dish cloth while you prepare the first batch of doughnuts.

Dust the work-top well with flour and drop the mixture on to it. Dredge with just a little flour and gently roll it out to about ½in thick. Using a floured glass or biscuit cutter about 2in in diameter, lightly press circles into half the dough, but do not actually cut it. Place a small teaspoonful of jam in the center of each. Cut out the same number of circles from the other half of the dough, and turn the top, unfloured sides over onto the jam circles.

Stick the doughnut edges well together (the jam must not leak out as they cook) and gently press around the edges with the end of a teaspoon handle. Cut out each pastry with a slightly smaller cutter. Turn over the finished doughnuts and place them well apart on a floured board, covering lightly with a dish cloth. Set the doughnuts to rise in a warm place (p. 149) and turn them over when they have risen on one side so that the other side may rise. Assemble the left-over scraps and beat them into the remaining dough with 2 spoonfuls of warm milk and finish in the same way.

A light and well-risen doughnut should have a pale ring around its middle, and the wider the ring, the lighter the pastry will be. Cook only four or five pastries at a time and always start by cooking the side that has risen first.

Heat the oil to 330-350°F. Using a large slotted spoon, gently lower each pastry into the hot oil at 4-second intervals. Watch them all the time for they brown very quickly. As soon as they have colored well, which takes about 2 minutes, flip each one over and cook the other side until it is golden brown.

Lift the doughnuts out of the oil, drain on kitchen paper for a minute or two and roll them in sugar. Serve the doughnuts while they are still warm, with a glass of white or red wine.

Strawberry Shortcake

Pastry

250g/2 cups plus 3 tbsp all-purpose flour, plus extra for dusting

2 tsp baking powder

½ tsp salt

pinch of nutmeg

50g/¼ cup sugar

65g/5 tbsp unsalted butter, chilled and cubed

1 egg

140ml/⅔ cup heavy cream or ½ cream and ½ milk

130g/9 tbsp unsalted butter, softened for spreading on cooked layers, plus extra for greasing

Fruit filling and topping

350g/12oz strawberries, redcurrants or raspberries

3 tbsp sugar

2 tbsp kirsch or Grand Marnier

250ml/9floz double or whipping cream

450°F for 20 minutes

This mouth-watering dessert should be eaten while it is still warm. Why not offer it after a light summer supper? The shortcake dough may be prepared 1-2 hours ahead of time and kept in a cool place. Have the butter, fruits and the cream ready too, so that the warm cake can be assembled in just a few minutes.

Reserve a few fruits for decoration. Slice 75g/⅔ cup strawberries but leave other fruits whole. Crush the rest of the fruit and stir in 2 tbsp of the sugar and 1 tbsp of the liqueur. Fold in the sliced fruit and set aside.

Sift together the flour, baking powder, salt, nutmeg and sugar into a bowl. Drop in the butter pieces and quickly rub to a crumb texture. Lightly beat the egg into the cream and pour on to the dry mixture. Combine quickly into a smooth dough. Butter and flour a 8½in spring-form pan and press in the dough. Bake and cook for a short time on a wire rack. Split the shortcake in two and spread half the butter on the bottom layer and the rest on the underside of the top layer. Spread the fruit filling over the bottom cake and sandwich with the top layer. It does not matter if the fruit oozes out.

Beat the cream until softly peaked and beat in the rest of the sugar and liqueur. Spoon the cream on to the shortcake and decorate with reserved fruits.

DOUGHNUTS: *A great American favorite served in the Old World with champagne on New Year's Eve or at the Shrove-tide carnival.*

Butterscotch Pie

165ml/5¹/₂floz milk
2in vanilla pod, split
140g/²/₃ cup light brown sugar
1¹/₂ tbsp potato flour or
*   cornstarch, sifted*
25g/3 tbsp all-purpose flour,
*   sifted*
165ml/²/₃ cup boiling water
40g/3 tbsp butter, softened
2 eggs, separated
¹/₂ tsp ground nutmeg
100g/³/₄ cup pecan nuts,
*   chopped small*
140ml/²/₃ cup whipped cream,
*   whipped and sweetened*
pecan halves to decorate
1 baked shortcrust pastry shell
*   8¹/₂in (p. 145)*

A rich dessert for those with a very sweet tooth!

Bring the milk and vanilla pod to the boil. Draw off the heat and leave to infuse for 15 minutes. Remove the pod. Mix together the brown sugar and flours. Stir in the boiling water and butter, then add the milk. Pour the mixture into a heat-proof bowl, or the top pan of a double-boiler, and set over a pan a quarter filled with simmering water.

Stir and cook the mixture until it has thickened. Cover with a lid and leave to cook for 10 minutes longer, giving it an occasional stir. Add the well-beaten egg yolks and cook for 1 minute more. Draw off the heat. Beat the egg whites until stiff; pour the hot mixture on to the egg snow and fold together, using a large metal spoon. Fold in the nutmeg and pecan nuts.

Pour the mixture into the baked pastry shell. Decorate with pecan halves. Chill well. Pipe whipped cream rosettes over the butterscotch filling and cut in wedges.

Chilled Sultana and Orange Cheesecake

1 cooked fat-free sponge
  24cm/9½in diameter
  (p.142)
75g/3oz candied orange and
  lemon peel, chopped
100g/3½oz sultanas
2 tbsp Grand Marnier or
  Cointreau
oil for greasing
25g/3 tbsp gelatine powder
300g/1⅓ cups curds cheese,
  sieved
75g/⅓ cup sugar
250g/1 cup lemon curd
2 tbsp orange zest
370ml/2⅔ cups heavy cream,
  softly whipped
5 tbsp chopped pistachios

Syrup

75g/⅓ cup sugar
25ml/2 tbsp water
3 tbsp Grand Marnier or
  Cointreau

140ml/⅔ cup whipping cream,
  whipped and sweetened
2 tbsp orange liqueur
candied peel and pistachios to
  decorate

Although the traditional baked cheesecakes, introduced from Europe, were favoured for many years, in recent times America has made the unbaked variation its own, and it has gained worldwide popularity. This confection is no longer a conventional cake but an elaborate dessert, more suitable for a special occasion or as the climax to an elegant dinner.

Soak the orange and lemon peel and the sultanas in Grand Marnier or Cointreau for at least 30 minutes. Make a syrup with the sugar and water boiled to thread stage (p.151). Mix in the liqueur. Cool.

Slice the sponge cake horizontally into two layers, of one-third and two-thirds thicknesses. Lightly oil a 9½in spring-form pan and line the base with wax paper. Drop the thicker cake layer into the pan and brush all over with the flavored syrup.

Sprinkle the gelatine on to 75ml/ ⅓ cup very hot, but not boiling, water in a cup and stir to dissolve. Leave to cool. The mixture should be transparent and lump-free, if it is not, place the cup in a pan of warm water and heat gently. Cool to room temperature before using. Meanwhile, beat the curds cheese with the sugar, lemon curd and orange zest until well blended. Gently trickle over the gelatine liquid, beating all the time.

Set aside until the cream is on the point of setting. Using a large metal spoon, lightly fold in the soaked peel and sultanas, the liqueur, whipped cream and the pistachios.

Pour the cheese filling on to the sponge cake in the prepared pan and smooth it out. Carefully cut half of the remaining sponge layer into six triangular pieces and evenly space them on top of the filling to create a fan effect.

Flavor 40ml/⅔ cup sweetened whipped cream with 2 tbsp of orange liqueur and pipe rosettes of cream on the cake. Decorate with candied peel and pistachios. Chill for 5-6 hours. The cake may be prepared 2-3 days ahead of time and kept in the refrigerator.

STRAWBERRY SHORTCAKE: *The shortcake pastry is very much like an English scone; the almost savory flavor is a perfect foil for sweet strawberries and whipped cream.*

AMERICAN CHEESE-CAKE: *This unbaked cheese filling, on a sponge base, is made of cream, curds cheese and lemon well-flavored with liqueur. Serve it for a special dessert.*

Basic Preparations

Beating egg whites and folding in

Egg whites expand almost three times in volume, and beating them correctly is possibly the most important basic technique in successful baking.

For best results, egg whites should be beaten in a large, spotlessly clean bowl (if necessary, rub it with half a lemon before rinsing and drying), and use either a balloon whisk or a hand-held electric mixer.

Begin beating only when you are ready to use the egg snow in the recipe, as, once beaten, the air is held for only a short time before the mixture collapses and turns to water. (When sugar is beaten into the egg snow the structure will hold for much longer before collapsing.) Once you have begun beating you must continue until the egg whites have fully expanded. Start by beating slowly, but as the whites begin to foam, increase the speed. Working in a figure-of-eight movement with the beaters, and rotating the bowl as you mix, cut down, round through the mixture and up high out of the bowl to incorporate as much air as possible. The mass will become thick and white, with firm, cream-colored peaks. Stop now. You should be able to invert the bowl and the whites will remain intact. If you beat any longer they will become granular, separate, turn to water and collapse. In this state they are unusable!

Folding in sugar and other ingredients by hand

The correct technique for folding in the aerated egg snow to the main cake mixture is almost as important as the whisking process. This is also the case when folding other ingredients into the egg snow itself.

The aim is to retain as much of the air as possible in the cellular structure of the beaten whites, and a light careful touch is essential. Folding in should always be done by hand, using a large metal spoon.

Tip about half the egg snow on to the main cake mixture. Then, making a figure-of-eight movement and rotating the bowl slowly, turn the spoon and fold the mixture over lightly, cutting down through to the bottom and up high into the air. Make sure that both mixtures are well blended but *never stir*. Continue until all the egg snow is used. The texture should be spongy and light but firm. Pour it into the prepared baking tin immediately, rap the tin smartly on the work-top once to burst any bubbles of air and place the tin in the preheated oven.

A meringue mixture

The same folding-in technique applies to a meringue mixture, but here the sugar and other ingredients are folded into the whipped snow.

The proportions for meringue are 1 egg white to 55g/¼ cup sugar. (A mixture using 2 egg whites makes a 8½in flat disc of meringue.)

Prepare a sheet of wax paper and on it trace a circle of the required size. Beat the egg whites until they stand in firm, creamy peaks; sift over half the sugar and continue beating until the mixture is stiff, smooth and shiny. Sift over the rest of the sugar, in two stages, and lightly fold it into the mixture.

Drop the meringue mixture on to the prepared wax paper, then, using a metal spatula, gently coax it into a circular disc about ¾in deep, taking care not to flatten it or lose the air that has been beaten into it. Smooth the surface lightly. Dry out immediately in a low oven (275°). It will take anything from 1½ to 3 hours to dry, depending on the size, and it will turn a very pale coffee color.

Test for readiness by gently tapping the underside of the meringue. If it sounds slightly hollow, it is ready; if not, leave to bake a little longer.

Meringues may be kept for several weeks wrapped in aluminum foil and stored in a dry, cool place.

1: Carefully separate the egg whites from the yolks, and drop them into a large spotlessly clean bowl.

2: Lightly beat the egg whites until they are foamy.

3: Continue beating more vigorously until the egg whites have expanded into firm creamy peaks about three times their original volume.

4: Sift half the sugar into the mixture and beat until it is smooth and shiny.

5: Gently fold in the rest of the sugar in two stages, using a large metal spoon.

6: Tip the meringue onto the prepared wax paper and lightly smooth it out using a large metal spatula.

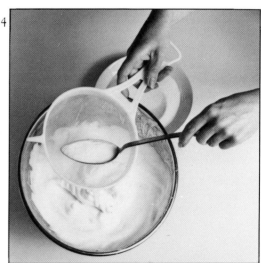

Fat-free sponge

For a 8¹/₂-9¹/₂in pan

4 whole eggs (200g/³/₄ cup)
100g/¹/₃ cup plus 1 tbsp sugar
2in vanilla pod, split
100g/³/₄ cup plus 1 tbsp flour,
  sifted

350° for 30-35 minutes for a
  deep cake or 20 minutes for
  a shallow cake

The classic method
The eggs are beaten over heat in this method. Use either a balloon whisk or a hand-held electric beater.

Lightly beat the eggs and sugar in a heat-proof bowl. Set the bowl over a pan a quarter filled with simmering water, ensuring that the base of the bowl does not touch the water. Continue beating the mixture as it warms for 5-10 minutes, until it has changed to a pale color and is rich and creamy in texture. Lift the bowl off the heat; carry on beating while it cools and until the volume has trebled and a thick ribbon of batter will drop off the beater and leave a trail in the mixture for at least 5 seconds. This takes about 20 minutes by hand or 10 minutes with the electric mixer. Lightly blend in the seeds of vanilla pod.

Sift over the flour and fold it in, in three stages. Using a large metal spoon, work in a figure-of-eight movement and lightly and quickly cut down sharply through the mixture and up again, rotating the bowl as you work. Never stir the mixture or the air will be lost and the cake will be heavy and damp.

When all the flour is incorporated and the mixture well blended, pour the batter straight into a prepared spring-form pan or into two shallow sandwich pans. Tap the pan on the work-top once to disperse any air pockets and bake immediately in the pre-heated oven.

When baked the cake should be well risen and golden in color, and it should shrink slightly from the sides of the pan. It will feel springy to the touch. If in doubt, insert a wooden cocktail stick or skewer in the middle of the cake; it should come out clean. If any mixture adheres, leave the cake in the oven for a few minutes longer.

Lift the cake out of the oven and leave to settle in the pan for 5 minutes on a wire rack. Run a knife around the inner edge of the pan to release the cake and unclip the spring side. Invert the cake on to another wire rack, remove the pan base and peel off the paper. Leave to cool.

The beaten egg white method
In this method separated egg whites are beaten into a firm snow and folded into the prepared, cold egg yolk batter with the flour. The finished cake is paler and lighter in texture than one made in the classic way.

Reserve 2 tbsp of sugar and beat the rest with the egg yolks in a large bowl until the mixture is creamy and white and falls in a thick ribbon from the whisk. This takes

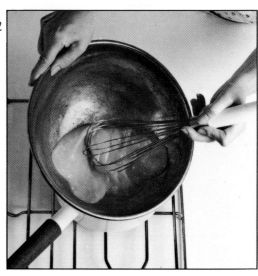

1: Place the sugar and whole eggs in a large bowl set over a pan a quarter filled with simmering water.

2: Lightly beat the mixture until it starts to foam and thicken.

3: Continue beating until the mixture is pale and creamy and has trebled in volume.

4: Take the bowl off the heat and continue beating until the mixture has cooled and thickened, and a ribbon trail of batter will remain on the mixture's surface for 5 seconds.

5: Sift one-third of the flour over the bowl.

6: Using a large metal spoon, gently gold in the flour, taking care not to lose any air in the mixture.

7: Sift and fold in the rest of the flour in two stages.

8: Scoop out the finished mixture into a lined, greased and floured baking pan.

3

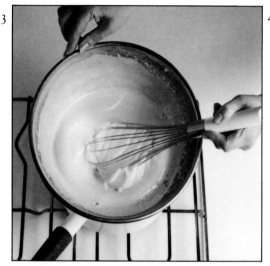

4

5

6

7

8

In this method the mixture is not warmed during preparation.

1: *Beat the egg yolks and sugar together until the mixture is pale and creamy and falls in a thick ribbon from the whisk . Beat the egg whites separately in a large bowl until they hold firm creamy peaks.*

2: *Tip one-third of the egg snow onto the egg yolk and sugar mixture and gently fold it in using a large metal spoon.*

3: *Sift one-third of the flour and gently fold it in.*

4: *Continue folding in the egg snow and flour in two further stages.*

5: *When all the ingredients are incorporated into the mixture it will be firm and well expanded.*

6: *Lightly scoop the mixture out of the bowl into the prepared baking pan.*

about 10 minutes by machine (15-20 minutes by hand). Beat the egg whites in a large bowl until they stand in soft snowy peaks. Sift over the reserved sugar and continue beating until the mixture is firm and glossy looking. Drop a third of the egg snow onto the egg-yyolk mixture and fold it in. Drop a third of the egg snow on to the egg yolk mixture and fold it in. Sift over one third of the flour and fold it in. Repeat in two further stages. Finish in the same way as for the classic method.

A fat-free sponge will keep fresh for 2-3 days. It will also freeze well for up to 2 months; defrost at room temperature for 2-3 hours.

Genoese sponge

For a 8¹/₂-9¹/₂in pan

4 whole eggs (200g/³/₄ cup)
120g/¹/₂ cup sugar
5cm/2in vanilla pod, split
120g/1 cup all-purpose flour,
*   sifted*
120g/¹/₂ cup butter, melted and
*   cooled*

350° for 45 minutes

This recipe is basically the same as the fat-free sponge but with the addition of butter. It has the advantage that it will keep fresh for up to a week.

The best genoese is composed of equal amounts of sugar, flour and butter. Use half the quantity of butter for a less rich cake.

Follow the directions for either of the fat-free sponge methods, but finish by folding in the melted butter into the prepared cake mixture in three stages, taking care to exclude the sediment in the bottom of the pan. Pour the batter into the prepared cake pan and bake.

Sweet shortcrust pastry

For a 8-8¹/₂in pan

120g/1 cup all-purpose flour,
*   sifted*
pinch salt
40g/3 tbsp sugar
¹/₂ tsp lemon zest
1 egg yolk
90g/7 tbsp butter, softened

For a 9¹/₂-10¹/₂in pan

150g/1¹/₂ cups minus 1 tbsp all-
*   purpose flour, sifted*
¹/₂ tsp salt
50g/¹/₄ cup sugar
1 tsp lemon zest
2 egg yolks
110g/¹/₂ cup butter, softened

To prepare by hand   Sift the flour and salt into a mound on the work-surface. Make a well in the center and drop in the sugar, lemon zest and egg yolk. Working with the tips of the fingers, lightly and quickly draw in a little flour from the edges and toss to combine until the sugar is absorbed. Add the butter pieces and blend all the ingredients together into a crumbly texture. Gather the pastry into a ball, it does not matter if butter pieces are still visible, and blend it on the work-surface by pushing away small portions of dough at a time, using the heel of the hand. Form the dough into a ball, wrap it in plastic film or aluminum foil and chill for at least 30 minutes before using.

Using an electric food processor   The butter should be chilled before use so that the pastry is less likely to be overworked and lose elasticity, which makes it tough.

Drop the flour, salt, lemon zest and chilled butter cubes into the processor bowl. Blend for 10-15 seconds to a fine crumb texture; coarse lumps mean that it has been over blended. Drop in the egg yolks and blend for a further 10 seconds until the dough forms a compact ball. Wrap and chill overnight.

I prefer to finish the pastry by hand after the first stage of blending. Turn the crumb mixture out on to the work-top and combine with the egg yolk. Blend together by kneading as in the hand method. Chill for half an hour before using.

Rolling out the pastry and lining pie and tart pans
Roll out the pastry on a lightly floured work-surface until it is about 2in larger than the pan. Leave it to rest for a few minutes so that the pastry loses some of its elasticity and will not shrink when you line the pan.

Lightly butter the baking utensil.

Lay the rolling pin across the middle of the pastry and gently fold the pastry over it. Lifting it carefully, lay the pastry over the prepared pan, taking care not to stretch it. (It may easily be patched if it breaks.) Ease it into the pan and smooth away any air-bubbles, working from the center to the edges. Trim off the excess flush with the edges, or leave a small border and crimp it up, by pressing the pastry, at regular intervals, with the back of a knife. Prick the base all over with a fork and leave to chill.

Crisp pastry base
To help crisp the base of the pastry, preheat a flat baking sheet and bake the tart on it.

Par-baking
Sometimes a pastry base needs to be partially baked before it is filled.

Prepare the pastry and line the pan, prick all over the base with a fork. Take a sheet of aluminum foil or wax paper larger than the cake tin and lightly press it into the pastry case, carefully pushing it up the sides. Make sure that it is tucked in closely to all the edges so that the pastry cannot collapse on the sides or rise as it bakes. Weigh it down with ceramic pastry pebbles, rice or dried beans.

Place on the hot baking sheet and bake in the pre-heated oven (400°) for 10-15 minutes until the pastry has just set and is barely colored. Remove from the oven and leave to cool for 4-5 minutes before removing the paper and weights.

Baking blind
An empty, baked pastry case is often needed, particularly for fruit fillings. Fluted metal tart pans with loose bases give the best results.

Prepare the pastry and line with paper or foil and pebbles as above. Place on the hot baking sheet and bake in the preheated oven (400°) for 10 minutes, then reduce the temperature (350°) and bake for a further 20 minutes or until the pastry is golden. Remove from the oven, lift off the paper and weights and brush the base with lightly beaten egg white (which will insulate the pastry from wet fillings and help prevent it from getting soggy). Replace the tart in the oven and bake to dry for 5 minutes more. Lift out of the oven and leave to cool in the pan on a wire rack.

1: Sift the flour and salt onto the work surface, make a well in the middle and drop in the sugar, lemon zest and egg yolks. Lightly blend the ingredients.

2: Add the butter pieces and continue to blend until it is crumbly in texture.

3: Gather the pastry into a ball.

4: Blend the pastry by brushing away small portions of dough at a time, using the heel of the hand.

1: Lightly roll out the pastry until it is about 2in longer than the tart pan. Leave the pastry to rest.

2: Drape the pastry over the rolling pin, carefully lift it up and lay it across the tart pan.

3: Gently ease the pastry into the tart pan.

4: Use the back of the hand to press the pastry into the base and sides of the pan.

5: Trim the surplus pastry from the top edges of the tart pan.

6: Prick the pastry base all over with a fork.

Classic puff pastry

For 500g/1lb pastry

200g/1³/₄ cups bread flour, sifted

¹/₂ tsp salt

25g/2 tbsp unsalted butter, softened

¹/₂ tsp lemon juice

75-125ml/¹/₃-¹/₂ cup chilled water

175g/³/₄ cup unsalted butter, chilled

425° (see also individual recipes)

Roll the puff pastry into a long rectangle, then fold over and overlap each end to form a square.

Always use unsalted butter for puff pastry, *never margarine.*

Basic dough   Sift the flour again with the salt into a large bowl. Cut in 20g softened butter and work together with the flour to a fine crumbed texture. Add the lemon juice and most of the water, and knead lightly into a firm dough; if it is too stiff, add more water. Gather into a ball and flatten slightly. Score the top crosswise with a knife. Close cover and leave to chill in the refrigerator for 2 hours.

Wrapping in the butter   The work-surface must be chilled to the same temperature as the ingredients. Use a marble slab or place a bag of ice-cubes on the work-top beforehand. Lay the cold butter between two large sheets of plastic wrap and lightly bat it with a rolling pin into a flattened, pliable 6in square.

Lightly flour the work-top and the rolling pin. Unwrap the chilled pastry and bat it two or three times to soften it slightly, then roll it out on the floured top into a 12in square. Place the square of butter in the center of the pastry square and wrap over the pastry sides to envelope it completely. Make sure that all the seams are well sealed by pressing gently with the rolling pin.

Rolling and folding the dough   Always keep the work-top and rolling pin lightly dusted with flour, but brush away any excess. Always roll away from you.

Lay the rolling pin across the dough about 1in in from the edge; never roll over the ends as the butter and trapped air may be squeezed out. Lightly roll the dough into a rectangle about 6 × 12in. Fold over and overlap each end into a square. This is the first fold. Turn the pastry by making a quarter turn to the right, so that the open ends are parallel to the rolling pin. Roll the pastry away from you as before and fold again into a square. This is the second fold. Turn the pastry another quarter turn and make a slight indentation in the side that is to be rolled next.

Carefully wrap the dough in plastic film and chill for 15-20 minutes. It is essential to allow the dough to rest so that it may relax and stretch when it is rolled. Lightly bat the dough two or three times to start it moving, then roll, fold and turn it twice more. Indent, wrap and chill again. Repeat this sequence once more and chill for 30 minutes.

In all you have made six folds and turns. The dough is now ready for use.

Raw puff pastry keeps in the freezer for up to 6 months. Defrost in the refrigerator overnight. If it has been finished for baking there is no need to defrost it; simply increase the basic baking time by about 5 minutes.

Raw puff pastry can be kept in the refrigerator, closely wrapped, for 3-4 days.

Yeast dough

Handling yeast

Fresh yeast gives the best results and can usually be bought in health-food shops and small bakeries. It should be beige-white, look creamy and moist in texture and cut in a block, rather than crumble.

Dried yeast comes in granular form. The concentration is twice that of fresh yeast: for instance, 30g/1oz (generous) = 15g/1 tbsp dried yeast. See the container for special instructions for preparation.

Bread or strong wheat flour gives a better rise to yeasted goods because it contains more gluten and will stretch more.

The main ingredients of a yeast cake and the utensils should all be slightly warmed before use, as yeast is encouraged to grow by heat; but the temperature must never exceed 80°F/25°C as greater heat kills the yeast cells.

Yeast pastries are usually prepared in three stages: an initial batter sponge, followed by two rising or proving periods. The dough is covered at these times and is set in a warm, draft-free place. An airing cupboard is ideal, or above the oven. I have two ovens and find the rising heat from the lower oven is sufficient to warm the upper oven. The dough should be left to rise in a large mixing bowl; remember it must increase to about double the volume. A large, lightly oiled plastic bag may also be used.

Preparing a yeast sponge batter

Warm the liquid to blood heat (80°F/25°C) as stated in the recipe and pour it into a jug or bowl. Crumble over the fresh yeast and stir. Add 1 tsp of sugar and about a quarter of the flour in the recipe and beat until smooth. Cover and leave to ferment for about 10 minutes. It should bubble and expand in volume to about twice the size. Make sure that the yeast has completely dissolved. If there is little or no action after about 20 minutes, the yeast is old. Throw it away and start with a new batch.

Kneading the dough

When the yeast has been incorporated with the other ingredients, the dough needs considerable beating and kneading to encourage the yeast activity and to give lightness and a fine texture. At first it will be rather sticky and difficult to handle, but the more it is worked the less sticky it will become. Finally it will detach itself entirely and roll off the sides of the bowl into a smooth, silky and elastic mass, showing large bubbles of air. At this point the dough is covered and left for its first proving.

When the dough has doubled in bulk it is knocked back — the air is punched out of it and it is kneaded for a minute or two longer. The remaining enriching ingredients, such as nuts, dried and crystallized fruits, are usually added at this stage. The dough is finished and placed in the warmed, buttered and floured baking utensil, and left for a further, shorter period of proving. It is then baked in a hot oven. See the individual recipes for temperatures.

Basic Creams and Fillings

Cooked vanilla custard cream — crème pâtissière

250ml/1 cup plus 2 tbsp milk
1½in vanilla pod, split
2 tbsp cornstarch
2 egg yolks
100g/7 tbsp unsalted butter,
  softened
50g/½ cup confectioners' sugar,
  sifted
1 tbsp rum or kirsch (optional)

Reserve 3 tbsp of milk. Bring the rest of the milk and the vanilla pod to the boil, draw off the heat and leave to infuse for 10 minutes. Whisk the cornstarch and egg yolks with the cold reserved milk. Remove the vanilla pod from the hot milk and stir the milk into the egg mixture. Pour the batter back into the pan and reheat the custard until it has thickened. Set aside to cool. Beat the unsalted butter and the confectioners' sugar until light and fluffy, then whip in the cold custard a tablespoon at a time. Mix in the rum or kirsch if used. Chill for at least 30 minutes. The custard may be kept in the refrigerator for 2-3 days or frozen for up to 1 month.
Chocolate and coffee flavor Melt 100g/3½oz bittersweet chocolate with 1 tbsp instant coffee and 1 tbsp water. Leave to cool. Blend into the finished custard.

Cooked egg yolk and buttercream

110g/½ cup sugar
100ml/7 tbsp water
5 egg yolks
2in vanilla pod, split
225g/1 cup unsalted butter,
  softened

Dissolve the sugar in the water in a heavy-based pan over gentle heat, then boil briskly to the thread stage (225°F; p.151). Lightly beat the egg yolks in a bowl and slowly pour on the sugar syrup; continue beating until the mixture has cooled and is light and fluffy. Mix in the seeds of vanilla. Beat the butter in another bowl and beat in the egg mixture a spoonful at a time. Leave to cool before beating in the flavor of your choice.

Chocolate and coffee flavor Melt and cool 100g/3½oz bittersweet chocolate. Dissolve 1 tbsp instant coffee into about ½ tsp boiling water. Stir together well before blending with the finished cream.
Mocha flavor Replace the water in the main recipe with very strong, fresh black coffee. Proceed as above. Add 1 tbsp rum.
Rum, kirsch or Grand Marnier flavour Adding 2 tbsp of any one of these liqueurs will give a good strong punch!

Basic buttercream

3 egg yolks
75g/¾ cup confectioners' sugar,
  sifted
200g/14 tbsp unsalted butter,
  softened

Combine all the ingredients and the chosen flavor together and beat until well blended and smooth. Chill for a short time.
Flavorings 2½ tbsp fresh lemon or orange juice, strained; *or* 2½tbsp liqueur, spirit or eau de vie (Grand Marnier, rum or kirsch); *or* 1 tbsp instant coffee dissolved in ½ tsp boiling water; *or* 100g/3½oz bittersweet chocolate, melted and cooled; *or* 1 tbsp cocoa powder.

Whipped chocolate cream

*250g/9oz finest bittersweet
   chocolate*
225ml/1 cup heavy cream
2in vanilla pod, split
*1 tbsp coffee liqueur or dark
   rum*

Break the chocolate into small pieces and drop them in a pan with the cream and vanilla seeds. Set the pan on a low heat and, stirring all the time, melt the chocolate and bring the mixture to a boil. Draw off the heat immediately. Pour the mixture into a large bowl and leave to cool, stirring from time to time to prevent a skin forming. When cool, add the liqueur or rum and beat vigorously until the mixture lightens and doubles in volume. Use immediately as the filling hardens very quickly.

Cooking sugar

Sugar syrup often forms the basis for icings and creams.

Granulated or preserving sugar and water are heated in a heavy-based pan or an unlined copper sugar pan. A sugar thermometer is used to measure the different temperatures. Keep the thermometer warm in a jug of hot water so that it will not crack when dipped in the boiling syrup. Use sugar and water in proportion of 500g/1lb: 150ml/ $^2/_3$ cup and a pinch of cream of tartar dissolved in 2 tsp water.

Pour the water into the pan and drop in the sugar. Set the pan over a very low heat, and warm gently until the sugar has dissolved. Stir carefully with a wooden spoon to avoid splashing the pan sides, as any sugary deposits that fall back into the syrup cause it to crystallize and prevent it from reaching the correct temperature. (Brush away and dissolve the crystals with a wet pastry brush if necessary.) When all the sugar has dissolved stir in the cream of tartar and bring the syrup to a boil. Stand the warmed sugar thermometer in the pan and read the measurements at eye level. Increase the heat and boil briskly until the correct temperature is reached.

Lift out the thermometer and immediately plunge the base of the pan in cold water for a moment to arrest further cooking. Use at once.

See individual recipes for further instructions.

Sugar temperatures
The boiling times given in this list are approximate.
Thread (102°C/215°F) 20 seconds. Dip scissor points in the syrup, open them and thin threads should form.
Pearl (104°C/221°F) 25 seconds. A stronger thread will break and form a small pearl-like drop on the end.
Feather and soft ball (115°C/240°F) 2-3 minutes. A little syrup dropped into chilled water can be shaped into a very soft, flattened ball.
Hard ball (120°C/250°F) Over 3 minutes. The ball is firmer in the water and holds its shape better, but is still a little soft.
Small crack (140°C/280°F) About $3^1/_2$ minutes. Forms a firm lump of sugar in the water, becomes brittle, then snaps.
Hard crack (155°C/310°F) 4 minutes. Dipped in cold water the sugar will break like glass.
Caramel (173°C/345°F) Boil the syrup until it is pale and amber colored. Cool immediately by plunging the pan base in cold water, or the caramel will start to smoke and blacken; it is too late to use it then.

Apricot jam glaze

A cake that is to be iced or covered with chocolate should first be brushed with a coating of strained apricot jam. The jam glaze both insulates the crumb surface and helps bind the covering to it.

Gently heat together 100g/7 tbsp apricot jam and 2 tbsp water. Boil until the mixture has thickened slightly. Press through a fine sieve. Brush the warm jam on the cake and leave to cool before proceeding.

Any remaining jam may be stored in an air-tight jar for later use.

Using a pastry bag

Fit a pastry bag with a piping nozzle. Lightly grasp the bag about half way down and flap the top edges back and down over your hand. Use a spatula or spoon to insert the filling in the bag, taking care not to soil the top edges. Fill the bag only about half full so that the mixture does not squeeze out of the top as you work.

Straighten up the top edges of the bag, while gently squeezing the filling down, and gather and twist them together to prevent the mixture from oozing out. Always squeeze down from the top. Refill the bag in the same way.

Piping bag, spatula and various nozzles for piping.

1: Push the piping nozzle firmly into the bottom of the pastry bag.

2: Fold the top of the pastry bag down over your hand.

3: Open out the center of the bag so that the spatula can be pushed in.

4: Push some of the buttercream filling into the bag.

5: Carefully draw up the folded edges of the pastry bag over the cream fillng; press the filling down gently and gather the end of the bag together; twist round.

6: Holding the pastry bag steady with one hand, exert gentle pressure with the other and pipe stars onto the iced cake surface.

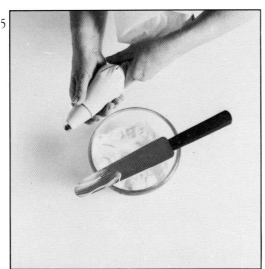

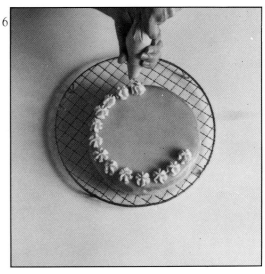

Fondant icing

For 500g/ 1lb icing

140ml/²/₃ cup water
450g/2 cups sugar
½ tsp lemon juice, strained

This is not as complicated to prepare as at first seems, and it does keep fresh for several months. If you make a large quantity it will always be on hand when you need it. Half the quantity is enough to cover a 8½-9½in cake. Pour the water into a heavy-based pan, or unlined copper sugar boiler; add the sugar and lemon juice. Heat gently until the sugar has all dissolved, then bring to the boil and cook briskly until the syrup reaches the soft ball stage (115°C/240°F); 2-3 minutes of boiling (p. 151). Pour the syrup straight on to a cold wet marble slab or wet work-top and leave to cool for 1 minute.

Using a wooden spatula or metal scraper, work all round the syrup, lifting it from the edges and slapping and folding it over into the middle. It will change from a clear transparent syrup to a dense creamy mass.

The syrup will now be cool enough to handle. Continue working — it will set hard otherwise — kneading and punching by hand, and folding in the same way as one handles dough. After about 10 minutes it should look matt white and feel smooth and firm.

Wrap in plastic wrap and leave to rest for 1 hour; or store in the refrigerator.

The fondant must be softened before use. Place the amount you need in a heat-proof bowl and set it over a pan half-filled with simmering water; in this instance the water may come up the sides of the bowl. Warm very gently and add just a little tepid water (about 2 tbsp is enough for 9oz fondant), for an unperfumed flavor. When the fondant mixture has the texture of thick cream it is ready for instant use.

To color the fondant, add a drop of vegetable coloring. For a spirituous flavor, use kirsch, dark rum or Grand Marnier instead of the water.

Strained lemon or orange juice gives a good citrus tang, while 2 tsp coffee extract or 1 tbsp instant coffee dissolved in 1 tsp boiling water gives coffee flavoring. For chocolate flavor add 2 tbsp cocoa powder, or melt 40g/ 1½oz chocolate and mix it with the thinned fondant. Fondant handles in much the same way as glacé icing. See below for the method of applying the icing to a cake.

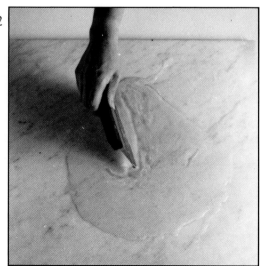

1: Pour the hot sugar syrup onto a cold damp surface — marble in this case.

2 and 3: Use a metal scraper and work all around the syrup, lifting from the edges and slapping and folding it into the middle.

4: The syrup is changing from a clear syrup to a dense opaque mass.

5 and 6: The fondant is creamy-colored and thicker in texture.

7: The fondant is much whiter and thick enough to be worked by hand.

8: The fondant has been kneaded to a smooth and firm texture. It is ready for use.

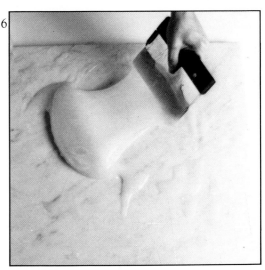

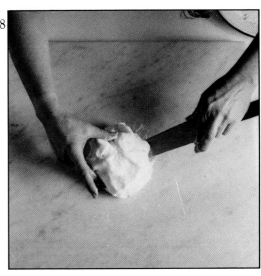

To ice a cake

Make sure that the cake is level by cutting away any unevenness. Stand it on a wire rack set over a sheet of wax paper, large enough to catch the drips. Brush off the excess cake crumbs, then brush the top and sides all over with warm apricot glaze; leave to cool while you prepare the icing.

Pour most of the icing on to the center of the cake and replace the bowl over the pan of hot water to keep it moist. Using a long dry spatula or knife and working from the middle outwards, quickly smooth out the icing with sweeping strokes and without allowing it to spill over the edges. Avoid the temptation of working over the surface again, for it will already have begun to set. Coat the sides of the cake with the rest of the icing. Immediately lay the prepared decorations in place.

Glacé icing should be allowed to dry first if it is to be piped with thicker icing or buttercream.

1: Brush the cake with strained apricot jam and then leave it to cool on the wire rack. Place the spatula in hot water.

2: Quickly pour the warmed icing over the cake, starting in the center and working outwards.

3: Tip the cake rack backwards and forwards so that the icing runs to the edges of the cake.

4: Finish the sides of the cake by smoothing on more icing, using a hot, dry spatula.

156

Glacé icing

Vanilla icing for a 8-8½in cake

200g/1¾ cups confectioners' sugar, sifted
2-3 tbsp water, almost boiling
4 drops vanilla extract or flavor as below

Vanilla icing for a 9½-10½in cake

250g/2¼ cups confectioners' sugar, sifted
4-5 tbsp water, almost boiling
5 drops vanilla extract or flavor as below

This simple icing is easy to prepare but a little tricky to handle. You have to work fast as it dries very quickly. Before making the icing prepare all the decorations and lay them out in exactly the pattern you plan to use.

Glacé icing starts to crack after about 4 days.

Flavorings Quantities given are for the smaller cake and should be adjusted for the larger. Use the liquid flavorings instead of water.
Orange 1-2 tbsp orange juice, strained
Lemon 2-3tbsp lemon juice, strained
Punch 1 tbsp orange juice, ½ tsp lemon juice, 2 tbsp rum.
Rum 3 tbsp rum, 1 tbsp water
Coffee 2 tsp coffee powder dissolved in 2½ tbsp water
Chocolate 2 tsp cocoa powder dissolved in 2½ tbsp water
Liqueur 2 tbsp liqueur (kirsch, Grand Marnier, etc), 1 tbsp water
To colour Dip a cocktail stick in the bottle of edible coloring and add to the icing one drop at a time; take care, as the color is very intense.

Method
Sieve the confectioners' sugar into a small, heat-proof bowl; make a well in the middle and gently and gradually stir in the water or flavorings using a wooden spoon. Avoid adding too much liquid at once or the icing will be too thin and runny. It should be smooth and thick, and creamy enough to coat the back of the spoon. If too thin, add more sugar; if too thick, add more liquid.

Set the bowl over a pan of simmering water, making sure that the base does not touch the water, and gently warm the icing so that it runs more easily when it is poured on the cake. Use straight away.

Thick chocolate icing

For a 8½-9½in cake.

100g/3½ bittersweet chocolate
½ tbsp unsalted butter
165ml/²/₃ cup water
100g/7 tbsp granulated water

Melt the chocolate and butter together with 1 tbsp of boiling water in a heat-proof bowl set over simmering water. Draw off the heat and stir to blend. Put the water in an unlined copper sugar boiler or heavy-based pan, add the sugar and boil to the thread stage (p. 151). Stir the chocolate liquid straight into the syrup and replace the pan on the heat. Boil gently for 5 minutes when the icing will have thickened. Test a few drops on a plate — it should feel sticky. Pour the icing straight over the apricot-glazed cake, tipping the wire rack back and forth so that the icing runs all over the top. Do not use a spatula on the surface, but smooth more on the sides. Decorate with fruits and nuts immediately, although piped decoration should be applied when the chocolate icing has cooled completely. The icing will set with a high gloss but will dull a little after 24 hours. The cake may then be stored in the refrigerator without spoiling.

Soft chocolate icing

100g/3½oz bittersweet chocolate
80g/³/₄ cup confectioners' sugar, sifted
40g/3 tbsp unsalted butter, cut in pieces
2 tbsp water

Melt the chocolate in a bowl set over simmering water. Stir in the sugar and the butter and continue stirring until the butter has melted and the mixture is smooth. Remove from the heat and add the water, 1 tbsp at a time. Use while lukewarm.

Do not touch!

Index

Picture Credits

Page 14 Topham Picture Library; page 14-5 The Image Bank; page 15 Mary Evans Picture Library; page 38 The Bridgeman Library; page 58 ZEFA; page 59 BBC Hulton Picture Library; page 86 Mary Evans Picture Library; page 88 BBC Hulton Picture Library; page 108 Swiss Tourist Board; page 110 Swiss Tourist Board (r) Mary Evans Picture Library (l); page 111 ZEFA; page 122 The Image Bank, Keystone Press Agency Ltd (inset l), The Image Bank (inset r).

Key   *(r) — right; (l) — left*